JOURNEY TO THE

Awakened Heart

ROBERT JACOBS

BALBOA.
PRESS
A DIVISION OF HAY HOUSE

Balboa Press books may be ordered through booksellers or by contacting:

Balboa Press
A Division of Hay House
1663 Liberty Drive
Bloomington, IN 47403
www.balboapress.com
1 (877) 407-4847

Print information available on the last page.

ISBN: 978-1-9822-1556-9 (sc)
ISBN: 978-1-9822-1558-3 (hc)
ISBN: 978-1-9822-1557-6 (e)

Library of Congress Control Number: 2018913326

Balboa Press rev. date: 11/09/2018

Contents

Part 1 The Outer Journey

Part 2 The Inner Journey

Part 3 The Journey Home

Dedication

I started to write this book for my children, who were then teens, curious about their dad's tales of his adventures in India, Morocco, and Paris. As I began writing, I started to relive the excitement of my early twenties when I traversed the planet in search of the meaning to my life. Looking back I marvel at my persistence and courage during those days. I never considered giving up my quest.

Recently I visited the Casa de Dom Inacio in Abadiania, Brazil, where I met several seekers in their late twenties and early thirties who exuded the same exuberance I had experienced in my early days. They too were seeking the deepest wisdom of their own selves and aspiring to lead lives that would allow them to serve humanity in the most profound way.

I felt a deep love for these seekers as I remembered my own uncertainties during my early years. Who was I really? What did I have to offer this world? Was I really destined to serve others? I certainly hoped so. Speaking with these seekers, I recognized that they too were facing the doubts and uncertainties that come with choosing paths that seem unusual and puzzling to family members and friends who wonder why spiritual matters are more interesting than pursuing promising careers.

So I write this book for the young people of today who are on the cusp of an expanded consciousness that I sincerely hope will bring balance to our planet, respect for our earth, and love for peoples of all races, nationalities, and creeds. May my story provide encouragement that if you seek, you will find; if you ask, it will be given; if you put forth effort, you will attain the desired fruits.

Finally, it is my hope that those reading this book will feel the profound blessings of my spiritual teachers, whose energies of grace have become part of my being and hopefully flow through the words of my book. May you all become friends with the divine light that lives within you. May you take refuge in your own innate wisdom. May you experience the most profound gratitude for the gift of your human life.

Introduction

It was a cold Monday evening, December 1, 1969, during a frigid winter in Cleveland, Ohio. A large group of us had gathered around the bar of the Commodore Hotel to await the news. Over the bar was an elevated television tuned to CBS News reporting from Selective Service headquarters, where the nation's first draft lottery was to occur. The service chief was about to dip his hand into a bowl of blue capsules that contained three hundred sixty six dates: the birthdates of the young men of America who were going to be drafted into the Vietnam War the following year. A low pick would assure being drafted immediately into the war. A higher pick offered hope that serving in a war most of us opposed could be avoided.

It was 7:00 p.m. and already dark outside. The bar was packed with students, men and women, downing beer after beer in a scene of anxious gaiety. Sitting at the bar, my eyes wandered to the long front windows that faced dreary Euclid Avenue where nighttime traffic rolled steadily by. Abruptly, it was announced that the lottery had begun and all eyes turned toward the television. The first birth date was announced: September 14. I could hear an anguished cry from the back of the bar and wondered who this unfortunate fellow was. It went on and on, birthdate after birthdate, until finally mine came up—March 19—on the two-hundredth pick. I felt a remarkable sense of relief that my pick was so late. I knew that there was still no guarantee I would not be drafted if I chose to give up my student deferment; nonetheless, a psychic space began to open around me that allowed me to consider the possibility of leaving school.

I was a smart Jewish kid from a good Jewish family and had been expected to become a doctor or a lawyer. My parents were from a small town in Pennsylvania and had lived through the Great Depression and World War II. My dad spent five years in the U.S. Army, serving in England and France in a capacity I was never clear about, although I asked him about it many times. I was a baby boomer, born three years after the war ended. My mother had eight miscarriages before I arrived, a hardship that even now I can barely comprehend. I once saw a photo of her taken shortly after my birth. She had the look of someone who had received a profound blessing from God. So I was special from the start; the one who survived. You might say I was spoiled, but I think more correctly that I was loved.

We were a middle-class family, not poor and not wealthy. My dad had been a buyer of carpets and floor coverings for a string of department stores, moving our family around the East and Midwest until he finally found his niche in western Pennsylvania shortly before I graduated from high school. I graduated third in my class and seemed destined for success. But it was during those years that something awoke in me that made me start questioning everything. Does God really exist? If he does, why can't I experience him? What is the purpose of human life? Why are there so few rich people and so many poor? Why are black people treated with such disdain? Why is my country bombing villagers in Vietnam? The list went on and on.

Growing up in my safe and secure home, there was a lot I was not exposed to. So I began to read books by those who had experienced the world quite differently. I read Malcolm X's *Autobiography*, Dostoevsky's *The Grand Inquisitor*, and J. D. Salinger's *Catcher in the Rye.* I began to ask questions about what life really meant. I eagerly anticipated studying philosophy in college and pictured myself discussing these issues with professors who were as intently interested in them as I was.

I chose to enroll at Case Western Reserve University in Cleveland, Ohio. My parents told me that it was a great school. My first year there I joined a fraternity of mostly Jewish kids, many from Long Island, and I quickly discovered that most were not remotely interested in the things I was. By the end of my freshman year, I had quit the fraternity and started adopting an alternative lifestyle, joining a group on campus that embraced the new hippie culture. Instead of sports coats and ties, we wore jeans and work shirts to class. We let our hair grow long and adopted a language with the new, unique hippie vocabulary. As time went on, we engaged in demonstrations against the Vietnam War and took over administration buildings. Things were changing quickly in American society and college campuses were at the center of the deep cultural changes sweeping across the country.

During my final two years in college, I rarely went to class. At one point I read a novel that profoundly affected me, *The Sound and the Fury* by William Faulkner. The title was taken from a line in Shakespeare's *Macbeth*: "Life is a tale told by an idiot, full of sound and fury, signifying nothing." The bleakness of these words and the somber feeling within the novel took me to a psychic place I had never before experienced. I felt an emptiness at the core of my existence that made the normal routines of my life seem superficial and meaningless. It took away whatever remaining motivation I had for doing what was necessary to get through college. If there was essentially no meaning to life, what did it matter if I earned an A in American Literature? Little did I know that this sense of emptiness was not far from a deeper emptiness that, instead of causing uncertainty and dismay, would leave me feeling profoundly fulfilled and satisfied with my life.

Still, in spite of forgoing my classes, I received a remarkable education at college. I voraciously read the authors and philosophers who inspired me: Faulkner, Joyce, Blake, Kierkegaard, Nietzsche, Marcuse, and many more. I devotedly studied what was interesting to me and left the normal formalities of college by the wayside. By the end of my four years, I had accumulated "incompletes" in all of the courses from my final three semesters. Yet I came out with a knowledge and exposure to literature, philosophy, and social sciences that I would later find almost unparalleled among my peers.

I had a wonderful group of friends in college who also embraced the new hippie lifestyle but somehow they were able to go to their classes, get good grades, and graduate with degrees. I often wondered how they were able to play by the rules of a culture I deemed superficial at best. It was something I had lost the ability to do.

So it was that I called it quits. The two-hundredth pick in the lottery had given me an excellent chance of avoiding the draft and I was ready to make my move. One morning I typed my resignation and dropped it off at the dean's office, leaving it on the desk of the dean's secretary. It read, "I, Robert Jacobs, hereby submit my resignation as a student at Case Western Reserve University. I now want to start learning about life."

I wasn't sure what my next step would be. During the past years, I had been most influenced by writers who had opened up a new world of possibilities for me. I began to think and hope that writing would be my calling as well. In my freshman year, I wrote a series of short stories called "Routines," which I shared with friends who were impressed by their novelty and humor. Throughout the rest of my college years, I continued to write and share these stories. Now it occurred to me that if I could experience life outside of the cloistered environment of college, I would be able to write about my experiences as did my heroes—Jean Genet, Samuel Beckett, James Joyce, and others. I knew that all of them had spent time in Paris where their creative juices had been nourished and had ultimately flourished. I decided that I too would go to Paris and gain the worldly experiences I needed to become a writer of their caliber.

On yet another cold winter day in Cleveland, I packed my belongings into my tiny Triumph Herald and drove home to speak with my parents about my intended travels. I was pretty sure they wouldn't be able to understand my motivations. Sitting with them at our kitchen table, I told them that I was quitting school and traveling to Paris to become a writer. My father blinked uncomprehendingly, disappointment clear in his eyes. Even my mother, who had valiantly tried to understand my unconventional behavior over the past four years, was glassy-eyed and confused. I felt for them both. It was difficult for me to explain to them what I was going through. I barely understood it myself.

So, out of compassion, I changed tactics. I told my parents I wanted to go to Israel and live on a kibbutz to explore my Jewish roots. This they understood! My father's eyes brightened at the idea, and my mother began to smile.

And so my journey began.

Part I

THE OUTER JOURNEY

Chapter 1

THE ROAD TO PARIS

It was shortly after my twenty-second birthday in March 1970 that I flew out of New York's Kennedy Airport, headed for Tel Aviv, with fifteen dollars in my pocket. My parents had no idea I had left with so little money. After landing in Tel Aviv, I easily found an office that placed young men and women on kibbutzim around Israel. I was assigned to one called Tzora, midway between Tel Aviv and Jerusalem.

It was a forty-minute bus ride to Tzora down the highway that connects Tel Aviv to Jerusalem. I was dropped on an isolated, country road that led to the kibbutz and walked the mile in with my heavy backpack, arriving in the late afternoon. Tzora was set on a wide expanse of rolling fields and orchards. On my way to the kibbutz office, I passed a cattle barn, some poultry pens, and a large area that was the living quarters for the residents.

Most of the residents of the kibbutz were Jewish expatriates from South Africa, older than I was and interested in little that was interesting to me. However, there were about fifteen men and women staying at the kibbutz from other countries—the U.S., U.K., the Netherlands, Brazil, Germany—who made life interesting. We had our meals together, worked together in the fields, and spent our evenings sharing stories of our home countries while passing around bottles of kosher wine. Some evenings a group of us hitchhiked into Tel Aviv for a night on the town. A café in Tel Aviv catered to the new hippie lifestyle and we flocked there as often as we could. I found no other such place in my time in Israel.

The kibbutz was a healthy break from my past four years stuck on an urban campus surrounded by the cold, gray ghetto of a decaying town. I enjoyed kibbutz life, getting up at four in the morning to feed the cows, working in the wide, sun-drenched fields, and setting irrigation pipes in the fields needing water. It was good physical work and I enjoyed my time with my fellow travelers but I was restless. Something deep within me had drawn me to take this trip and Paris was my intended destination. I wanted to be a writer. I wanted to know myself and have experiences that would help me find meaning in my life. It seemed that the writers I most admired had spent time in Paris; their experiences there had transformed them and given them the direction they needed. I hoped the alchemy of living in Paris would have the same effect on me.

So, early one morning, after a month on the kibbutz, I said goodbye to my friends, grabbed my bags, and walked the mile back to the highway, where I caught a bus to Jerusalem. Before heading to Paris, I needed funds, my fifteen dollars having long since disappeared. In Jerusalem I found a labor office that placed newly-arrived immigrants. After I answered their most important question correctly—yes, I am a Jew!—I was immediately placed on a job putting up telephone wires in a new section of the city. The work was not difficult. I worked with a crew of six other immigrants from a variety of countries who did what a crew of three could have easily done. I worked there long enough to buy passage on a ship to Greece, with a bit more to last until I could find work in Europe.

Greece was beautiful and cheap and I easily got by on a few dollars a day. I roamed Athens for a week and then took a boat to Crete to explore the island. I hitchhiked across the island to a secluded beach near the town of Vai, on the far western tip, where I carved out an area for my sleeping bag and pack—my room on the beach! There was a group of travelers living there and a tiny restaurant that provided fresh meals and Greek wine. For a week I swam each day and hiked through the countryside. Nearby I found an old, whitewashed Greek Orthodox monastery built around a beautiful courtyard garden filled with flowering bushes and vines. There were only three remaining monks and they were all over eighty. I was fascinated by this beautiful spiritual refuge and found it sad that soon there would be no one left to care for this unique place.

After my week of sun and beach, I started focusing on getting to Paris. My funds were almost gone and I did not want to arrive in Paris without money so I headed to Munich to find work on a U.S. Army base. I hitchhiked through Greece, at each stop writing quotations by Samuel Beckett on traffic signs. I hoped someone would read them. I managed to hitch a ride on a slow-moving train through Austria and eventually made my way into Germany.

A cool and rainy afternoon greeted me on my arrival to Munich. I navigated my way to Schwabing, the hip student section of town near the University of Munich, one of Europe's oldest universities. There, on the wide boulevard near the University, I met a strikingly beautiful, young German woman named Signe who, seeing my backpack and hippie attire, excitedly approached me, assuming I was like one of her heroes—Jack Kerouac. I was reluctant to disappoint her so I briefly recounted my recent travels with some clever exaggerations to make me sound more Kerouac-like. Impressed, she invited me to spend the night at her apartment, where I stayed for a few days.

Being with Signe I was reminded that, along with my search for meaning, I was also searching for a kindred female. In this respect my college years had been disappointing and at times downright depressing. I longed for intimate female company but my confusion about life and my own identity somehow seemed to block what I was looking for. Most of the women I dated or spent time with at college could not relate to my persistent questioning about life, leaving me feeling the odd man out. Many of my friends seemed to easily find relationships.

Upon meeting Signe I hoped that something special would develop between us. She was fascinated by my life on the road and introduced me to her set of friends. They were also fascinated by the Beat writers and seemed to identify me with them. They were also intrigued by the new hippie lifestyle that was just coming to Europe. Signe took me to the home of two of her friends, a pair of architecture students named Kiki and Koko, who had plenty of room in their apartment and offered me a place to stay while I worked in Munich.

The four of us spent many hours together sharing our desires for interesting, exciting, and meaningful lives. They seemed to envy my freedom and my daring to travel wherever I wished. Yet, though they found my choices exciting, they were happy and secure in their university lives. It did not occur to them that they could deviate from their set paths. Again I found a gulf between myself and my friends. Somehow I was always the one who broke from the normal path and sought something different. Because of this gulf, I realized that my relationship with Signe would not go far. I was roaming a bit further off the path than most college students felt safe to go. And I recognized that my inner discontentment would make it difficult for Signe or any woman to stay with me for long if she did not share the same inner longing. I was, after all, wandering this planet because, deep within, I felt incomplete and only occasionally happy. So far life had not seemed to offer me what I needed to be truly content. I wondered what woman would want to hang out with a guy who was, at his core, so dissatisfied.

I took a job for a month at the U.S. Army base in Munich, washing dishes at the main commissary. Finally, after earning what I took to be sufficient funds, I was ready to depart for Paris. On my last night in Munich, Signe, Kiki, and Koko threw a goodbye party for me and, the next morning, drove me to the highway to see me off. It was sad saying goodbye to them. It had been great to have such good friends. I didn't know when I would again connect with such a *sympathique* group.

I hitchhiked for most of that day, catching one ride after another. Eventually I found myself at an intersection of highways in southern France, where I was stuck for several hours. I began to despair that I would ever get a ride. Finally, a young American driving a tiny sports car stopped and gestured wildly for me to get in. I jumped into the front seat and, as we took off, found out we were headed for Spain, not Paris. I decided this was not a time to be inflexible. I agreed to accompany him through Barcelona and Madrid for a few days before we headed back to Paris. My new friend's name was Tom and he was a Stanford student taking his summer off to travel around Europe. He'd heard that Spain was cheap in these Franco days and was curious to see what it was like. I remembered that the writer Genet had lived in the barrios of Barcelona, which had provided inspiration for his writings. We eventually found a *pension* in Barcelona near the old barrios and explored the church of Gaudi. Then we found an equally cheap pension in downtown Madrid and spent a couple of nights there enjoying the food and wine. Spain was fun but Paris was on the horizon.

I don't know why I was certain that Paris would be special for me but I was not mistaken. We finally pulled into Paris on a sunny afternoon in June. Our destination was the Left Bank, the intellectual and artistic seat of Paris, where artists and writers had gathered for years. We drove into the Latin Quarter and parked our car just off the Place Saint-Michel, a block from the river Seine. Spotting a couple of Americans sitting in a cafe nearby, we joined them for a glass of wine. It was a beautiful spring day. The trees along the Boulevard Saint-Michel were in full blossom. I sat in the outdoor cafe surrounded by the sights, smells, and sounds of the Latin Quarter and the excitement of finally being in Paris took over my thoughts and feelings.

The two Americans we sat with were students from Princeton, also spending the summer in Paris. David was a tall, soft-spoken man with a warm smile and twinkling eyes. His friend Len, also outgoing and intelligent, had been crippled by a childhood bout of polio that left him wearing heavy metal leg braces and walking with crutches. His arms and shoulders were enormously strong. Both were friendly, perceptive, and open to my sense of humor, which bonded me to them immediately. David had just rented a studio apartment on a narrow cobblestone street called Rue Saint-André des Arts, a block from the Place Saint-Michel, and invited us to crash there until we found other lodgings.

David's apartment was small, with just a living room and a kitchen, but big enough for several people to sleep on the floor in sleeping bags. Within a few days, eleven of us were living in that studio apartment as more fellow travelers joined our enthusiastic group. From the start the group was international, with young men and women travelers from the U.S., the Netherlands, England, Germany, Sweden, Denmark, and Brazil. A crazy chemistry united us as we roamed the streets and neighborhoods of Paris, had picnics on the Seine, and rejoiced in the springtime vibes of Paris in its most beautiful, intoxicating season.

After two weeks in David's apartment, the landlord discovered that eleven of us were living there and evicted us. Remarkably, that same day we all found rooms at Cité Universitaire, a large complex of dormitories in the southern part of Paris built after World War II for international students. Since it was summer and school was out, rooms were readily available at low student prices. I gambled and spent the rest of what I had earned in Munich for a room in the Maison des États-Unis for the remaining three months of summer.

Tom, David, Len, and others who had joined our circle also moved into rooms on the Cité grounds.

Cité Universitaire lay directly across from the sprawling and forested Parc Montsouris and was set on spacious grounds with beautiful lawns and gardens that surrounded our dormitory buildings. Several pathways ran behind the dormitories through the gardens connecting the buildings to athletic fields and cafeterias. I had a bright, spacious room in the Maison des États-Unis and, within a few days, a group of other fellow travelers was encamped in my room with their sleeping bags. The Cité dorms became a destination for young international travelers that summer and appeared to attract every interesting hippie who was visiting Paris.

Hippie culture was at its peak in the spring of 1970. Many of the travelers who converged on Paris that summer with their communal spirit of love, peace, and rock and roll sought out like-minded souls to enjoy the goodwill that flowed so easily in those days. After paying my summer's rent for my room, I had completely exhausted my funds. One of the members of our group was a Danish man named Sven who sang and played guitar. The two of us started playing together at night on one of the narrow tourist-filled streets in the Latin Quarter to make some money. Many of our group joined us there and played kazoos and simple percussive instruments to back up our music.

After playing a few nights, we found that the best way to attract a crowd was to buy a few bottles of wine early in the evening and pass them around as tourists came to see what was going on. As Sven and I started singing and playing, our friends passed around a hat, soliciting francs from appreciative and tipsy onlookers. Our repertoire was small: a couple of Dylan songs, a few by Neil Young, and a couple of cowboy songs that the French thought were very funny. We took in a lot of francs that summer just having fun. A few times the crowd around us swelled to completely block the street and the gendarmes had to come to keep the traffic moving. We performed nearly every night that summer and managed to make sure that everyone in our group had enough money for their daily meals, metro fares, and cafés au lait.

Although our nights were always group events, I began to spend some of my days by myself, exploring on foot the unique neighborhoods of Paris. I spent a lot of time in the Latin Quarter and soon became a fixture at the Shakespeare and Company bookstore, run by an old American expat named George who had intimately known many of the writers I most admired—Hemingway, Joyce, and Beckett. His parlor above the bookstore had many autographed photos of the writers who used to hang out and live there and I spent hours at the store in my own studies of these writers. Across the bridge from the bookstore was the Notre-Dame Cathedral, facing the river Seine, that magnificent river that meanders through Paris, dividing it geographically and culturally into east and west banks. Along the river were walking paths dotted with bookstands, merchants selling their wares, and artists busily painting the picturesque scenes along the river.

During those months I read the works of Henry Miller and Anais Nin, who had lived and written in Paris in the 20s, and I sought out the locales they wrote about. Sitting in the parks in the Latin Quarter, I contemplated how to write of my own exploits in Paris. But I wasn't yet ready to begin writing. I was more interested in absorbing all that life in Paris had to offer. I was still unsure of what voice I would assume in writing about my experiences.

I became close friends with David and Len that summer as the three of us explored the nooks and crannies of Paris. Once again, however, I seemed to be the wildcard in our group of friends, the one who stretched the limits a little more, who took more risks than the others. It had been this way in college, where my friends marveled at how I could so flagrantly skip classes and try to live up to my idealistic visions of what life should be. For my friends these months in Paris were an adventure; for me Paris was more than just a summer vacation. I wanted it to be a way of life, one that would open up life's mysteries to me. David and Len and the rest would be returning to college after the summer, but that was not my plan.

And then there was Connie, a pretty blonde American girl also staying at the Maison des États-Unis who somehow always seemed to be there for me late at night after everyone else had gone to sleep. We would sneak into the gardens of the Cité grounds with our sleeping bags and spend the nights lovemaking under the stars. We didn't speak much to each other and during the days we rarely saw each other. But at night we fulfilled those basic human needs that were important to us, regardless of how little we really knew of each other. Our relationship that summer pretty accurately reflected my ability, or lack thereof, to relate to a woman on an intimate level. It was either sensual or intellectual but not both.

During the summer I learned that the Selective Service had drafted men up to lottery number one hundred ninety-five in the month of May but would draft no further. I had escaped it by five. I no longer had to worry about Vietnam and was no longer subject to the draft. I was immensely relieved.

My plan was to remain in Paris but, as with all plans, events unfolded in their own way. In mid-August our group started making plans to return home. David, Len, and Tom were returning to college. Sven and his girlfriend left for Denmark. In my heart I wanted to stay in Paris but I had very little money left from our musical performances and I would soon have to leave my room at the Cité. I felt torn. I didn't know where I would live in Paris or how I could continue to make money and all of my friends were leaving. On the other hand, I had no idea what I would do if I returned to the States and did not relish the prospect of returning to my studies.

Finally, drawn by David's encouragement, I decided to return to the States. My time in Paris had come to an end. I hitchhiked with him to London and bought a cheap flight back to the U.S. But I knew my travels were not over.

Chapter 2

THE HEART OF AFRICA:
SIERRA LEONE

I t took me over a year to get back to Paris. On my return to the States, I enrolled in college again, somehow believing that I would go to classes and try to pass them after two years of avoiding them. Within a few weeks, I recognized I'd made a huge error and had again wasted my parents' money. In December, I left school for good and took off for California with some friends. I spent a few months wandering around Berkeley and Big Sur before heading back to Boston for the summer. I didn't know what to do with myself. The inspiration that flowed through me during my travels in Europe had dwindled to a trickle.

One afternoon in Boston, I was eating lunch at an apartment where I was staying when a friend came in looking nervous and worried. He had somehow come into possession of a large amount of an illegal, mood-altering substance from Thailand and was intensely worried that he would get caught with it. I surprised myself by telling him I would sell it for him if he would split the proceeds with me. He immediately agreed.

I made a phone call to a college friend in Cleveland and the next day flew to Cleveland with the illegal substance in my carry-on. Two days later I was back in Boston with more money than I had ever had. I knew this had been a rash thing to do. If I had been caught, I would have been in big trouble. But I did it and for the first time in my young adult life I had enough funds to live for an extended period of time. Within two months I was on a plane back to Paris.

I arrived in Paris on a quiet summer evening in July 1971 and immediately headed to the Shakespeare and Company bookstore to check their bulletin board for a place to stay. The summer air was warm, the Latin Quarter was filled with tourists, and I was happy to be back. Already I could feel inspiration starting to flow back into my blood. As I looked over the bulletin board, I was approached by a tall French hippie with long red curly hair. He was accompanied by a cute, petite, young woman who was half his size. He said, "Hey man, you need a place to sleep? You can stay with us. My parents are out of town and we have their house to ourselves for a couple of weeks." I was not sure what to say. I was not exactly ready to commit myself so I told them I'd call the next day. Their names were Francois and Nicole and I made sure I had their phone number.

It was getting late, so I took the métro to Cité Universitaire, where I knew I'd be able to sleep in the gardens. It was wonderful sleeping under the stars again but when I awoke I came to grips with the fact that I no longer had a room at the Cité where I could take a shower. And a Cité breakfast was no longer an option. Not knowing where to turn, I called my new French friend who gave me directions to his home in the north of Paris, near Porte de Clignancourt.

Francois's family home was a beautiful two-story apartment just north of the big flea market at Clignancourt. I stayed there for two weeks while his parents vacationed and then the three of us moved to a smaller flat in the working-class neighborhood of Guy Môquet. Once out of the affluent setting of Francois' parents' home, I began to feel more at ease with my surroundings in Paris. Our apartment was a cold-water flat on the first floor of an older building with a toilet in the courtyard. The ceilings were high, the trim ornate, the kitchen simple but workable. We slept on foam mattresses and had little in the way of furniture. In short, it was perfect. I had brought my guitar from America and each evening I played from the rock and folk repertoire of the day.

I became close friends with Francois and Nicole. Francois's English was basic and at that time my French was almost nonexistent. We formed our own unique language of phrases that were neither accurate English nor French but which we both understood. Francois was intelligent and creative and he bristled at the restrictions of the French Catholic culture in which he had been raised. He was artistic and loved working with his hands. Nicole was diminutive and looked like a schoolgirl in her black skirt and white blouse. She had short dark hair and a trace of freckles on her pretty face. She was also artistic and sensitive and shared Francois' distaste for the repressiveness of French bourgeois culture. Both had been involved in the Paris student uprisings in 1968, which was still a rallying point for many young French.

I spent my days exploring Paris on my own as both Francois and Nicole worked at their day jobs. On the Left Bank's Boulevard Raspail, I started to frequent the American Cultural Center, a beautiful center dedicated to the many American artists who had lived in Paris over the years. It was directed for several years by the black American writer James Baldwin who turned it into a mecca for black American and French-African artists, especially jazz musicians. I had always loved jazz. I saw it as a unique art form that expressed, movingly, both the pain of human existence—particularly African American existence—and the beauty that always accompanies that pain.

I loved living in Paris and was excited by my exploration of life as an expat. Yet, as carefree as my life seemed, I had my own share of mental pain—the pain of not knowing how to fit into life, not understanding my own culture, not knowing what I should do with my life. I wondered who I was and if I would ever be lucky enough to offer something worthwhile to life. I certainly wanted to. Perhaps this is why I felt at home there in Paris at the American Cultural Center with the African American expats: Sonny Murray, a jazz drummer who had his own quartet; Steve Potts, a saxophonist who could do all of Coltrane's runs; Bobby Few, a pianist who had played with the experimental sax player Albert Ayler; and Alain Silva, a Frenchman of African descent who organized his Celestial Communications Orchestra, combining Europe's best jazz musicians with the American expats. All of these artists were talented, creative musicians who, except for Silva, had found America to be an inhospitable environment in which to live and grow. They expressed the same sense of disenfranchisement with their own culture that I too felt.

Slowly the Paris summer began to slip away and make way for autumn. Paris in autumn is very different from Paris in the summer. Gone were the tourists and large numbers of international travelers looking for fun, romance, and adventure, leaving me astonished to find myself in a Paris full of French people. I had not bothered to learn much French during my previous stay in Paris but now I knew that, if I wished to make Paris my home, I had to learn the language. Yet the thought of studying in a school-like environment was unpalatable. My experiences as a college student were still too close at hand.

For the first time in my travels, I had some money to do things. At first I thought of buying a car to travel around Europe, or even to India, but all the cars I found in my price range seemed on the brink of collapse. Francois, Nicole, and I spent many evenings discussing what my next step should be. I did not have the correct visa to work legally in Paris and was frankly not interested in taking on a menial job. I had some interest in a new school in Paris, the University of

Vincennes, which was the hub of new radical philosophies that had merged the psychoanalytic theories of Freud with the social theories of Marx, but I had little confidence that my French was good enough to understand the lectures or do the reading. I shared my situation with Francois and Nicole and they suggested I use my funds to explore the world while using Paris as a home base. They would always have an apartment where I could stay.

After a few weeks of thought, I decided to visit an old friend living in Sierra Leone, West Africa as a Peace Corps volunteer. Ken was one of my best childhood friends. We had much in common. A smart and inquisitive Jewish kid, he was a talented musician who taught me how to play guitar when I was fourteen. Together we formed our school's first rock band. Now we were both world explorers and neither of us felt at home in our own culture. I had always seen Ken as a deep thinker, unafraid of separating himself from the groupthink of our day. Whereas I had become a hippie and student radical in college, Ken had followed his own unique, indefinable path. He was different from anyone I knew.

Since Ken was in Sierra Leone, I thought this would be a great starting point for a longer trip through West Africa. I planned to fly into Freetown, the capital, spend a few weeks with Ken and then travel overland through West Africa to Lagos, Nigeria. From there I intended to fly back to Paris. Within a few weeks, I obtained all the necessary visas, got several vaccinations, and booked my flight to Sierra Leone.

I flew out of Paris in September 1971 and landed in the hot, humid Freetown Airport across the river from the town of Freetown. I brought a small pack, my sleeping bag, and my guitar. Remarkably, the only way to get from the airport to the city was by a ferry—really more like a rowboat—that crossed the wide Niger River where it emptied into the bay on which Freetown was built. Riding on the river and smelling the natural fragrances of Africa, I felt a deep recognition and remembrance of Mother Africa within me. I felt I had been there before. In Freetown I was befriended by a couple of street kids who led me to the City Hotel, a two-story wooden structure with a bar and restaurant sporting large wicker ceiling fans on the first floor. The rooms were on the top floor, the beds all enclosed by mosquito nets. The City Hotel retained the atmosphere of British colonial Africa even though the British had long since departed. It was owned by a Lebanese man, Sami, who kept it scrupulously clean. It was the best hotel in town for the small number of Westerners who visited the country.

Freetown was small and I was able to walk everywhere I needed to go. Without difficulty I located the Peace Corps office and found that Ken was living in a remote town in the southeastern part of the country, a two-day drive from Freetown. Before starting my trip, I spent a few days exploring Freetown and learning Krio, the native vernacular that mixes English with the local African dialects. I was led around town by a couple of young Freetowners who were happy to show me the city as well as their homes and how they lived.

Finally, I took a lorry across the rugged, barely paved roads that traversed Sierra Leone into the heart of the country. We passed towns and villages with colorful shops and kids running and playing in the streets. At our stops kids would come up to me and touch my hair, surprised by its strange texture. Many had never seen a white man before. By evening we reached the town of Kenema, where we stayed for the night at a small hotel. It was hot and humid and the beds were covered by the ubiquitous mosquito nets. After a good night's sleep, we were off the next morning to Segbwema, a town of two intersecting streets lined with simple homes and shops, where Ken was living. I found him at one of the two Peace Corp houses in the town, a simple but elegant wooden bungalow where four Peace Corp workers lived, attended by an African cook and a small house staff of African boys.

Ken was incredulous to learn that I had flown to Africa to pay him a visit and was enthusiastic to share his unique experiences. It was evident that he loved the outdoor life of rural Africa and was in his element. Although most of the Peace Corps volunteers stationed in Segbwema lived in one of the Peace Corps houses, Ken had moved into a smaller village of mud huts with thatched roofs about three miles from town on an unpaved road. The village was called Pendembu. There he dedicated himself to learning the local language, Mende, an unwritten, tonal language in which the pitch of the syllables affects the meaning of the words. The Africans loved Ken. He told me that, at first, they laughed at his attempts to speak their language, insisting that only an African could speak Mende. But after Ken returned from a three-week trip to America to visit his family, he found himself speaking Mende fluently. The villagers were shocked and Ken became a local legend.

Village life in Africa fit Ken's character so well that he seemed more at home there than in America. One of the village women cooked his meals in the rural African fashion and an old fisherman had taught him to fish with a net in the traditional way of his tribe. I saw that Ken was beloved by the African villagers because he related to each person in a kind, personal way. He gave all of the villagers his full attention, letting each see how important they were to him. In turn they also extended their love to me, his good friend. Many thought we were brothers, probably because of our similar Jewish features. Yet Ken and I shared something deeper, an innate curiosity about the mysteries of life and a desire to find the common bond we intuitively knew existed between all beings. At heart this is what bonded me to Ken when we were teenagers. We were brothers in the spiritual sense. In Pendembu we spent hours discussing where our lives were heading and trying to grasp the significance of what we were experiencing. In the evenings we returned to the pattern of our teen years, playing guitar and singing the songs of the 60s, drawing in the villagers each evening to listen raptly to our music.

Spending nights in Ken's mud hut and eating the "rice chop" prepared by the village women, I felt eerily at home. Here I was, three hundred miles into the heartland of Africa, surrounded by non-literate people who spoke an unwritten tonal language I could not understand. I was, for the first time, living without electricity or running water. Yet it all felt so normal.

I spent a month in Segbwema, staying some nights at the Peace Corps bungalow and others in Ken's hut in Pendembu. I became friends with the other Peace Corps volunteers and also with Mustafa, a young African man who worked at the Peace Corps house. At age fifteen he was reading Shakespeare and professing his love for English literature. One of the Peace Corps volunteers, Allen, had a long-term relationship with an African woman from Segbwema and had fathered a child by her. His Peace Corps salary, a mere stipend for Americans, was a fortune in Sierra Leone. Allen easily supported both his partner and their son with his earnings. While I was there, he chose to extend his stay for an additional year, putting off the decision of whether to marry his partner and bring her and their son back to the States.

One day I learned that there was an opening for a teacher at the school where Ken taught. After learning about me through Ken, the principal offered me the job for a year. The position included a monthly salary, my own small house in Segbwema, a cook, and a housekeeper. It seemed like an offer I couldn't refuse. There was, however, one catch. In order to take the job, I had to return to Freetown and change my tourist visa into a working visa. Thus, early the next morning, I hired a lorry to retrace my steps back across the rugged country roads of Sierra Leone to Freetown.

There was only one government building in Freetown and it held the office that issued visas for foreigners and visitors. The visa minister was a gracious, white-bearded, older African man who wore a military uniform that appeared to be from the nineteenth century. He had great difficulty understanding why I wanted to teach at the school in Segbwema. He pulled out the visa papers I had signed when I had arrived in Sierra Leone on which I had written for profession: "none." I explained that I wrote "none" on the visa forms because I had been in France as a tourist before making my trip to Sierra Leone. I then told him—falsely—that I had a college degree and was fully trained as a teacher in America. He didn't buy any of it; he denied my visa and gave me one week to leave Sierra Leone.

I was disappointed I couldn't talk this kindly man into giving me the visa I needed. I wondered why he was not open to someone like me, an educated Westerner, who wanted to teach village kids how to read and write. But I had to admit that I was not altogether displeased with his decision. Was I truly ready to take on the responsibility of teaching those kids for a full year? I didn't really know. I had never made such a commitment.

Reluctantly, I hired another lorry back to Segbwema to give my goodbyes to Ken and my Peace Corps friends and to inform the principal I could not work at his school. Ken was sorry I wouldn't be staying but was more concerned that I not overstay the week the minister had given me to leave the country. Ken told me that if I did not leave on time I could be put in a Freetown jail. He also said it would be much too dangerous to travel overland through West Africa to Nigeria. Besides the presence of bandits who preyed on travelers, it was unlikely I could make the trip without contracting an unwelcome tropical disease.

With those sobering considerations, I said my goodbyes to Ken, took a lorry back to Freetown, and booked a flight to Paris, leaving a day before my visa expired.

Chapter 3

MOROCCO

The inner city of Rabat was known as the Medina. It was surrounded by high walls and accessible through several gates that led back and forth from the old city to the new. The new city reminded me of Paris, with its cafés and wide streets and taxis. But the Medina was another world: narrow streets lined with shops; stalls stacked high with fresh dates, rings of dried figs, oranges, and mint leaves; and open-air tea shops with Arabic music blaring onto the streets. Moroccan men in their long, hooded *jalabas* filled the streets with bustling activity and noise. The melodic, throaty sound of Arabic permeated the air, a beautiful sound unfamiliar to my ears but comforting in its earthiness.

It was November 1971, early winter in Morocco, but still warm and sunny. I had returned to Paris from Sierra Leone and spent several weeks with Francois and Nicole before deciding to head south again. Winter in Paris was gray, chilly, and damp, and I yearned for the sunshine. Francois and Nicole recommended Morocco and I started to make plans for the trip. I found that, for a nominal fee, I could join a group of hippies driving a van to Tangiers.

As a gift for my departure, Francois took me to a fashionable English bookstore near the Champs-Élysées and purchased an English version of a book well-known in France, *Return to the Source*, by the Sardinian mystic Lanza del Vasto. Francois told me that all French young people knew of Lanza del Vasto, a follower of Gandhi, who led fasts and other acts of peaceful resistance during the French-Algerian civil war. I left Paris with *Return to the Source* carefully packed in my bag, saving it for when I settled in Morocco.

I arrived in Rabat late one afternoon after a train ride from Tangiers. Entering the Medina I looked for other Western travelers who could point me to suitable accommodations. Eventually, I spotted two hippie travelers at a tea shop off the main street of the Medina. Ned was an Englishman who had been in Morocco for only a few days but who had already been robbed of his money and belongings by a gang of thieves. Luckily, the English consulate had agreed to fly him back to England and he was leaving the next day. Juan was a young Costa Rican from a wealthy family who was traveling to "find himself" before taking up the mantle of his family's businesses and social standing in his home country. Like many of the Western travelers I met in Morocco, Juan was seeking something deeper and more fulfilling than the traditional role his parents expected of him in Costa Rica.

As we spoke over our mint teas, I gazed distractedly at the street and noticed a pretty Western woman walking past. She was graceful and slim with red hair and a smiling, thoughtful face. She wore a short, open black skirt that billowed in the air. In an instant Ned was out of his seat chasing this woman down the street. Within moments he was back, excitedly introducing me to this mysterious woman. This was Jo from Australia, a world wanderer, a friend with whom Ned had planned several months ago in England to meet here in Rabat and travel Morocco. But Ned had suffered the misfortune of being robbed in Morocco and could no longer accompany Jo on their intended travels. So it was, after awkward apologies by Ned, that young red-haired Jo, with her charming freckles and smiling face, became my traveling companion.

Rabat's youth hostel lay on a broad street directly outside the Medina and a block from the beach. It was a bright and airy place with a common room for meals and separate dormitory rooms for men and women. Here Jo and I took refuge after exploring the Medina and made our plans for discovering Morocco. Our first night at the hostel proved symbolic of how our relationship would proceed. After spending the day together, laughing and joking our way around the Medina and exploring Rabat's long, white-sanded beach, I began to feel a close relationship developing with Jo. That evening, past dinner, I was in Jo's dormitory room, a large, mostly bare room with bunk beds adjacent to each wall. Since Jo was the only woman in the room that evening, we were alone with no thought of the time. The hostel closed its doors at 10:00 p.m. and enforced a strict curfew. While talking quietly with Jo, I suddenly heard the door close and the lock click shut. Not realizing I was in the room, the hostel manager had locked us in the room at ten.

My first thought was that I was destined to have a romantic evening with Jo. But it didn't work out that way. Jo became noticeably nervous when it dawned on her that we were alone for the evening. As a pretty female traveling through Europe to Morocco, she had been forced into compromising situations with her male traveling companions and was still suffering from it. Valuing our nascent bond, with no desire to force myself on her, I quickly diffused her fear. In this way I assumed the role of Jo's friend, although I was already half in love with her. Oddly, that night, with only one blanket in the room, we slept together on a small bunk bed, sharing that single blanket. It turned out to be a chaste night, a night of friendship.

Moroccan towns were full of street hustlers who earned their living on tourists unfamiliar with the exotic ways of Morocco. Larabi was a Moroccan man in his late forties who had learned English while serving in the military during the Second World War. He was the consummate street hustler and a great guide who knew every corner of the Medina and where to find the best food, supplies, and clothes at the best prices. With Larabi accompanying us, Jo and I and our growing circle of friends were spared the higher prices usually offered Western tourists. While most Westerners ate at restaurants designed for the tourist trade, Larabi introduced us to local Moroccan haunts within the Medina that served incredibly good but simple fare. Sitting on wooden benches in small cave-like rooms beside working-class Moroccans, we were introduced to common Moroccan meals of couscous, *tagine*, thick soups with seasoned chunks of lamb, and freshly baked loaves of Moroccan bread. I had rarely found food so satisfying.

Within days of our arrival in Rabat, a sizable group of Western travelers had formed, all looking for a more remote and peaceful place in which to settle. After a few days of research and discussions, a group of five, including Jo and myself, decided to try the coastal town of Essaouira, an old Moroccan port town on the Atlantic coast just north of the vast desert region of southern Morocco. Others from our group pledged to join us later after they explored more of Morocco. It was a peaceful five-hour bus ride down the coast from Rabat to Essaouira, interrupted by stops in Casablanca and several smaller towns and villages along the way where Moroccans peddled and displayed their goods and foods on blankets and stalls at simple bus stations.

Essaouira was an important port city in eighteenth-century Morocco fronting a large natural harbor and surrounded by imposing walls. It was built as a fortress open only to the sea with several gates leading in and out of the town. It had a main square sporting its largest hotel and cafe, the Hotel Marrakech, and a few large intersecting streets that originated from the several city gates. Smaller winding streets, large enough only for foot traffic, wandered off from the main thoroughfares, sprinkled with traditional Moroccan homes built around open courtyards, mosques, small shops, and street vendors. These smaller streets offered an intimate view of the lives of ordinary Moroccan families.

Entering Essaouira we were led to the home of a Moroccan realtor named M. Levi who, we were told, dealt with the best properties in town. M. Levi was an older Jewish man, barely five feet tall but with ample girth, whose home was an apartment on the second, top story of a building on Essaouira's main street. We met at his large, ornate dining room table, which reminded me of the Passover tables my own family used in celebration of the Jewish holiday, and we discussed the properties he was renting. After I informed M. Levi that I was Jewish—and proved it to him by reading sections of his bible in Hebrew—M. Levi joyfully offered what he assured us was the best house in town for the price of three hundred *dirhams*, or sixty dollars, per month. We took it.

The house was located on Rue Ibn Khaldoun, a winding cobblestone street next to a mosque and across the street from a school. The entry was recessed from the street and opened into a spacious tiled courtyard with a fountain at its center, surrounded by the whitewashed inner walls of the three-storied structure. The ground floor held a kitchen and a large room that served as living quarters for a family of three. Upstairs, on the second floor, were two other larger rooms overlooking the courtyard, which were soon to be inhabited by Jo and Sarah, a young American woman who had joined us in Rabat, and Andrew and Jose, two travelers we met in Essaouira. On the whitewashed open roof was a smaller room I claimed as my own, with an open doorway and a bare, open window.

The travelers who joined us on Rue Ibn Khaldoun were also seekers, each in their own unique ways. Jo was the daughter of an Australian judge and had been living in Amsterdam for the past two years. She had already been exposed to the spiritual teachings of Meher Baba, an Indian mystic and yogi who embraced both the Hindu and Muslim mystic traditions. She was familiar with spiritual concepts I had not yet encountered. Like us all, Jo was searching for something she had not yet found in herself or in her life in Australia, something she hoped would form a foundation of meaning for her life.

Jose, an architect and poet from Argentina, was a small, thin man in his early forties with dark black hair, a goatee, and warm, glistening dark eyes that displayed his sensitivity and compassionate nature. He was recently divorced and was traveling the world to find a deeper meaning that his marriage and successful professional career had not seemed to offer him. After his stay in Essaouira, Jose planned to join an auto caravan to cross the Sahara into Mali and travel through Central Africa.

Andrew, Jose's roommate, was a tall American Jewish man in his early twenties with long brown hair and a long, full beard that made him look like Jesus, especially when he wore his *jalaba*. Andrew appeared "spiritual" in the naive way of most of us at that time who were beginning to explore spirituality, sometimes confusing outer expressions of spirituality for actual spiritual growth. Andrew often greeted others with a warm and emphatic "We are one!" followed by a big bear hug. Yet, as I grew to know Andrew, I discovered that he was a very smart young man whose spiritual instincts were deep-rooted and sincere. He, like the rest of us, was seeking that next step that follows the initial fascination and interest in spiritual ideas.

Joel was a psychologist from La Jolla, California, who came to Morocco with his wife Jean. Unlike most in our group, Joel was already a successful professional in his late twenties. Yet his story was intriguing. When he was nineteen and a college student in Brooklyn, he had an overwhelming urge to travel to Japan and live in a Zen monastery. He had no previous knowledge of Zen nor did he understand why he wanted to go to this monastery. Yet the urging was so strong that he did travel to Kyoto and spent a year living in a Zen monastery. Even after returning to the States, he told me he was unsure why he had gone to Japan or what he had learned there. The whole experience was puzzling to him. His travels to Morocco were a means to extricate himself from the normal routines of his life so he could better understand what really motivated and drove him from the inside.

Perhaps the most interesting member of our group was a handsome, intelligent Moroccan man named Abdulsalem who quickly befriended our group and offered us the inimitable hospitality that is so central to Arabic culture. Abdulsalem confided that he was involved in an underground political movement to bring political, economic, and social equality to the many Moroccans who lived in poverty, without access to meaningful education or economic opportunities. He was open-hearted and effusive in extending his hospitality to us, offering us traditional Moroccan meals and allowing us to partake in several religious celebrations with him and his family.

This was the core of our group that was open to many others who came and went through Essaouira. Soon our home served as a common meeting place for fellow seekers. Jo and I wandered the streets and alleys of Essaouira daily, stopping at shops, trying out restaurants and cafes, and walking the beaches. We became a common sight in Essaouira and most Moroccans and Westerners alike saw us as a couple. I was aware, however, that we were not a couple, just friends.

At this time I began reading Lanza del Vasto's book, *Return to the Source*. Lanza was a Sardinian who traveled to India in 1937 on a spiritual pilgrimage to meet and learn from Mahatma Gandhi. Shortly after he arrived in India by boat, his money and clothes were stolen and he gladly assumed the role of an Indian *sadhu*, a wandering mendicant who traveled India by foot, stopping at temples along the way for food and a place to sleep. His hard-earned poverty proved liberating for him as he, for the first time, learned to fully place his trust in God to take care of his needs. His poetic writings describe his wanderings and realizations as he traveled through India and finally met Gandhi at his ashram in Wardha, where he was allowed to stay and learn for several months.

One of the lessons Lanza learned in India was of nonattachment, a new concept for me. Gandhi taught that the inner self of all humans is of the same essence as the Absolute, or God, and that real happiness is based on discovering this inner identity with God, rather than trying to find fulfillment outside oneself. For this reason, during his time in India, Lanza practiced many forms of nonattachment, including poverty and selfless service, to enhance his spiritual growth. Lanza also practiced celibacy during his time with Gandhi, preferring to see women as his mother or sister so he could focus his efforts on deriving his happiness from his own being rather than focusing on what others could offer him.

As a twenty-three-year-old American male in those hippie days, Lanza's writings opened a door to a possibility I had never considered. For the past few years, I had been unable to sort out or understand all the confusing emotional, physical, and spiritual needs that motivated my relationships with women. On the one hand, I desired a relationship with someone who shared my values and was seeking something deeper in life, as I was. On the other hand, I had an acute desire just to enjoy myself with a woman, whatever the depth of the relationship. I was very sensitive to how I felt women perceived me and often overcompensated by coming on too strong. Spending more and more time with Jo, I again became aware of these impulses and the same confusing mixture of emotional and physical needs. There was no doubt that I was already infatuated with Jo and that I desired a relationship with her. But I realized that I had to learn how to better relate to women and move to something based more on the higher ideals I was reading about in Lanza's book. I understood that there was something much more significant in a relationship between a man and woman than just the common physical needs that everyone experienced.

So, I decided to try, however awkwardly, to inject the values I learned from Lanza and Gandhi into my relationship with Jo. For a starter I tried to see myself as being full and complete in myself, as a giver, as someone who serves others, not someone who needed recognition or a particular type of love from her. Gradually my relationship with her that winter became the cauldron for the first spiritual growth I attempted in my life.

My Argentinian friend Jose told me I was a fool, that I was denying my basic sexual and emotional needs for partnership, and that what I was doing was a form of sexual repression. But I sensed something important in my new stance that had to do with more than my relationships with women. It had to do with how I related to everything: myself, my friends and family, the world I lived in, and even with God. Something in Gandhi's teachings resonated with me at a deep level. Finally, I had a glimpse of what I had been searching for these many years: a means to live in this world with a true and compassionate love for all as its basis. I could barely believe my good luck at finding Lanza's book and determined that I would go ahead with my experiment with Jo.

My rooftop room became a refuge for introspection. As winter approached and the days grew shorter and cooler, living on the roof seemed like living in nature. I was surrounded by the open, star-filled Moroccan sky and the sounds and smells of the great Atlantic, its salt breezes and fresh ocean fragrances easily penetrating the open door and window to my room. I spent many hours on that roof, alone or with companions, sharing the magnificent presence of the ocean and stars, which silently formed a mystical and natural support for my spiritual longings.

In fact, all of Essaouira seemed to offer this support. On stormy days I climbed to the top of the city walls bordering the ocean and exalted as the waves smashed into the rocks and walls and sprayed cold filaments of seawater over the walls and onto the streets. The waves seemed relentless as they surged toward the walls, swirling in an ocean of blues and reds and purples, mirroring the same blues and reds of the storm-filled sky. The nature of Essaouira penetrated me like nothing else and exposed me to a deep mystical force that I now felt had its roots in my own being. Slowly the words of Lanza del Vasto and Gandhi began to take concrete shape in my experiences of the natural world. Nature, I was discovering, was a profound mystical force that nourished and reflected the same mystical force within me.

I also developed a growing bond and appreciation for the Moroccans with whom I lived and dealt on a daily basis. At the southern gate that led through the walls of the city into Essaouira was a café, carved out of the stone of the city walls. It was open all night and served hot coffees and teas, along with delicate Moroccan pastries. In the early mornings, from 2:00 a.m. onward, Moroccan farmers and traders began to enter Essaouira through this gate, bringing their foods and wares on donkeys and camels for the morning market. I often sat at the café during these early morning hours and watched the slow train of goods and people pass into the city. The beautiful, natural simplicity of these Moroccans touched something deep inside me. The simplicity of earning one's livelihood with the work of one's own hands was quite foreign to me and appeared to me to be an acceptance of God's world as is was that I had not yet experienced. Using my very basic Arabic, I spoke with these traders and farmers as they wandered into the town and shared coffee and biscuits with them before the morning sun rose to signal a new day.

My daily routine in Essaouira varied little. I awoke early in the morning from the sun shining through my open window and headed to the public bathhouse for a steaming hot bath. Few homes in Essaouira had hot water and ours was not an exception. Then I joined a large group of friends for breakfast at the outdoor café of the Hotel Marrakech, on Essaouira's central square. Often Jo accompanied me. By December the mornings in Essaouira were chilly but the brisk morning sea air always invigorated us. No one ever suggested having breakfast indoors. It was at this café and not in France that I became hooked on café au lait and numerous, delicious French pastries. It was also here, in the great comfort of our own good company, that my friends and I shared with each other the deepest longings of our hearts.

In this way I spent three months in Essaouira as the full thrust of winter settled onto the town, lowering the temperatures so that coats and hats were always a necessity during the days. Finally, one evening, eating dinner at a restaurant with Jo, she indicated, in her mischievous way, that she would like to engage with me as a man and woman that night. Although I didn't say so, inside I knew it was too late for me to have that type of interaction with her. I was still infatuated with Jo and the picture of her face was not often far from my mind. Yet something had changed in me through my growing awareness that I could offer love out of a feeling of my own fullness and expect nothing in return. This seemed to be the lesson I had learned from my relationship with Jo and it meant a lot to me. We had a wonderful meal and then walked the streets together as the sun went down over the city walls but when we returned to our home we both knew the moment had passed. What we had shared was indeed love, but love of a sort neither of us had known before.

Our visas for Morocco were good for three months, so in February, with winter still in force, we all made our separate plans to depart. Jose went off to his caravan to cross the Sahara. Andrew made plans to travel to Israel. Jo was undecided but thought she might return to Amsterdam. We all shared our addresses and phone numbers but as world travelers we were not sure we would see each other again. On a cold Moroccan morning in February 1972, I left Essaouira, where my spiritual search truly began. I hopped on a bus to Rabat and then managed to get a seat on a train that went all the way back to Paris.

Chapter 4

COMMUNAUTÉ DE L'ARCHE

I arrived in Paris early in the morning at the Gare de l'Est station after my all-night train ride through Spain and France. The métro from Gare de l'Est to Guy Môquet, where Francois and Nicole were living, was already crowded with Arab and Turkish workers who, it seemed, performed most of the basic labor in Paris. There was not much space for both me and my bags but I noticed a free seat next to a young woman I took to be French.

We spoke a bit and I found out that her name was Anne and that she was not French but American. She was spending several months in Paris as an *au pair* for a wealthy French family in a luxury apartment in the fashionable 2nd arrondissement. She and the other household help in the apartment building were given generously-sized rooms in the servants' quarters on the top floors of the building with a wonderful view of the city. She was friendly and attractive and I made sure before I exited the métro that I had her address and phone number so we could meet again.

Neither Francois nor Nicole were at the apartment when I arrived so I retreated back to the métro to search for Anne's apartment. I was familiar with Paris by now and easily found her building. I intended to leave her a note, thinking she would be at work, but to my surprise it was her day off and she was delighted to see me.

I had learned a lot from my relationship with Jo in Morocco but was not interested in a platonic relationship with Anne. I was ready for a truly intimate relationship with a woman. That first day in Paris together, we traversed the city, had café au laits and croissants in a nearby café, and eventually found our way to Montmartre, the hilly, picturesque northern section of Paris where several of the great Impressionist painters had lived and worked. We slipped into a small park there and, out of sight from passers-by, began kissing and having an intimate time. We eventually made our way back to her room, where we made love and spent the night together. Throughout the next few weeks, we were inseparable and Anne soon became close with Francois and Nicole.

My relationship with Anne softened the edge of loneliness that had been present throughout my travels, despite the friendships I had made. But there was still a more fundamental spiritual yearning within me that even a good relationship could not satisfy. In Morocco I had discovered something that connected me to the pure love existing within me. Having tasted that love, my heart ached to experience it more. I still carried *Return to the Source* with me for inspiration and knew from the book that Lanza del Vasto had established a spiritual community in the mountains of southern France. I shared with Anne my desire to visit this community and she encouraged me to go there. I was happy that she didn't feel threatened when my spiritual yearnings led me away from her.

So, just weeks after meeting the first woman in years with whom I had a fulfilling relationship, I took to the road again. I hitchhiked out of Paris to the town of St. Etienne in southern France to find

Lanza's spiritual community. It was early March, the weather gray and chilly. It took a full day to reach St. Etienne, a beautiful medieval town in the mountainous Massif Central region of southern France. It was too late to start looking for Lanza's community, so I had dinner at a local café and then searched for a place to sleep. Off the main street, I found a small park protected by a stone wall that provided a bit of privacy and slept there in my sleeping bag under a towering oak tree.

That night it began to rain heavily. At about 2:00 a.m. I had to gather my things and rush for shelter in the town. Soaked to the skin, I retreated under the awning of a café and sat on the cold, damp sidewalk, waiting for the night to end. Finally, the café opened early in the morning and the proprietor, seeing how cold and wet I was, warmly invited me in. I sat for several hours near the radiator, trying to remove the dampness from my clothes and bring some warmth into my body.

After breakfast the proprietor guided me to the local prelate who he thought would know where I could find Lanza's community. I easily found the prelate in his offices at the historic, medieval church and introduced myself. He was a gracious, intelligent man with a full, dark beard, dressed in the habit of his order. From the start he showed a lot of kindness toward me. He knew that Lanza del Vasto had established his Communauté de l'Arche outside of St. Etienne several years before but had since moved the community to a mountainous region farther south, near the town of Lôdeve. Concerned that I would not be able to find it, he spent over an hour making phone calls to locate l'Arche and finally made a reservation for me to stay there for a week. I left feeling extremely grateful to this man for his patience and sincere interest. It confirmed my feeling that if I traveled with a pure heart, I would find kind, open-hearted people who would guide me on my way.

Following the prelate's directions, I hitchhiked to Lôdeve that afternoon, having no trouble finding rides. Lôdeve was a picturesque mountain town, really a village, seemingly carved out of the mountains it rests in. It had so much natural beauty that I started fantasizing about living there. In the town, I found a café where I made inquiries about how to reach l'Arche. The patron of the café was familiar with l'Arche and had been there many times. Fearing that I would not be able to make it before nightfall, he magnanimously offered to drive me there that evening. I arrived at l'Arche after sunset and was warmly welcomed by the community.

Almost immediately the rugged simplicity and beauty of l'Arche evoked feelings of awe and respect in me. It was a converted seventeenth-century monastery, restored with immaculate craftsmanship, set in the midst of the rugged and wild Borie Noble mountain range. Far from the vestiges of modern civilization, nature prevailed, and its force and beauty were evident wherever I gazed. The buildings were made of fine stonework. There was no electricity and running water was just being introduced. I later learned that all of the work was done by hand, without the use of machines. It was an austere environment but only in the sense that nature itself is austere. For all its simplicity, the community seemed to lack nothing. The power of nature permeated the grounds and buildings of l'Arche and it appeared that the companions of the community devoted themselves to serving and blending in with the natural attributes of their surroundings.

There were about eighty companions of the community at the time, most of them well-educated French or Europeans, many having led professional lives before taking refuge in the spiritual lifestyle of l'Arche. All were committed to the Gandhian values of performing one's labor with one's own hands. The men plowed, planted, and harvested the fields without modern machinery, built and maintained all of the buildings on the property, chopped wood to keep the buildings warm, and hauled water in buckets from the well to provide drinking and bath water for the community. Much of the food was grown in their own fields and prepared in the l'Arche kitchen by the women, including fresh grains and vegetables and several varieties of country breads and cheeses. The women also made homespun cotton clothing for the companions. The community was almost entirely self-sufficient. Aside from the emphasis on physical labor, many parts of the day were set aside for meditation, prayer, and contemplation.

Lanza himself was an impressive figure, a tall, well-built man of over seventy years, with long white hair and beard, wearing the coarse homespun clothes that the community members wore. He had a kind face that always seemed to show the beginnings of a smile. During my first days at l'Arche, I did not speak with him directly but observed how he moved about the community with dignity and grace. He was often accompanied by his wife, a joyful older woman, tall and slim, who also played a large role in overseeing the community.

The men at l'Arche were strong and disciplined from their rugged work. Some good-naturedly poked fun at me for tiring while chopping firewood. The entire community was harmonious and everyone displayed reverence and respect for Lanza, who had conceived of the community and provided its spiritual inspiration. I felt welcomed by the companions and enjoyed the hard work and spiritual practices. Inwardly I hoped I would find my answer here at l'Arche and discover a deeper purpose. The setting seemed perfect for me and the spiritual ideals that motivated and guided the companions seemed exactly what I was looking for.

One evening after dinner, we all sat together to sing hymns. Since I had come with my guitar, several companions urged me to play folk songs from the civil rights movement of the 60s. They asked me to play "We Shall Overcome," which I awkwardly translated into French so they could understand the words. But seeing their serious faces, I could not resist joking around with the translation and soon all were laughing hysterically at my words. I marveled at the looks on their faces when they realized that I was joking about songs they held sacred. It was the first time I felt the companions truly open up to me. It was a precious moment.

Yet soon I realized that even this beautiful lifestyle was not in harmony with my particular spiritual needs. Although I valued the hard outdoor manual labor and the close bonds within the community, I found it difficult to relate in an authentic way with the l'Arche companions, who were mostly older than I and did not share the unique attributes of the hippie generation I was strongly a part of. I related most to the handful of young visitors at l'Arche who, like me, manifested the youthful exuberance of my generation. More profoundly, I found a certain element missing that I could not fully identify, a spark that would somehow undeniably draw me to it as if I had finally found home.

At the end of my week's stay, I was able to have a long talk with Lanza. He guided me to a secluded garden off the main building where we sat on two fallen logs, facing each other, his kind, piercing eyes examining me. After hearing about my travels and spiritual pursuits, he advised me simply to find a path before I was thirty and then follow it with complete determination. I was hoping he would see something in me that would lead him to ask me to stay longer, but he did not. I was reluctant to leave this man whose spiritual teachings had lit a fire within me, but my week was up and I had no choice but to move on.

On my last morning, I packed my bags, bid goodbye to my l'Arche friends, and hiked out through the mountains to a spot where a train stopped daily on its way to the town of St. Fleur. The day was cold and crisp, the mountains rugged and wild. I suddenly felt lonely and wondered where my path would lead. How many more mountain paths would I tread before I found the place that would satisfy my heart's longing?

It took me longer than expected to get back to Paris. The train to St. Fleur had few passengers as it cut slowly through the mountains, giving me ample time to contemplate my week at l'Arche. I arrived at the St. Fleur train station before noon and quickly walked through the town to the outskirts of the city, where I tried to hitchhike for several hours. Surrounded by the rolling hills and vineyards of the French countryside, I took the time to appreciate its beauty. But sadly, after several hours, I had to wearily retrace my steps back into town. I knew my remaining funds were not enough for a train ride all the way to Paris and I was undecided how to proceed. Wandering on the main street, I stopped to rest on a stoop leading to a small church.

I must have looked awfully despondent because a nun came down from the church and invited me in for tea and pastries. She was pretty in her dark habit, with sparkling blue eyes reflecting something special that I believed was her love of God. She could not have been much older than I was. She asked where I was going and I shared my travels to l'Arche and my spiritual quest; she listened with patience and kindness. I could see she was moved by my desire for a spiritual life. She spoke of her relationship to Jesus in a personal way and I was touched by her sincerity. Then, unexpectedly, she prepared a dinner for me to take on my way and walked me to the train station. To my great surprise, she bought a train ticket for me all the way to Paris. I was so moved by her kindness that I could barely express my gratitude.

I rode the train all night to Paris and didn't sleep at all. The effect of the nun's generosity moved me beyond words and all night I contemplated her kindness. I wondered how I could proceed in my spiritual search so that I too could be filled with such compassion for my fellow human beings. Contemplating these feelings I recognized that, ever since reading *Return to the Source*, I knew that one day I would make a pilgrimage to India. Now perhaps I was ready to make that journey.

Chapter 5

THE SILK ROAD: TRAVELING CENTRAL ASIA

I arrived in Paris the next morning and headed to Anne's apartment, where I found her getting ready for work. I told her about my experience with the nun and about my wish to travel to India. I asked if she wanted to travel with me overland to India and, to my surprise, she said yes. I was glad. It would be nice to have company on this long, difficult journey and I was not ready to give up my chance for a closer relationship with her. After a few weeks of preparation, we decided to hitchhike from Paris to Istanbul and then take trains and buses to India. We told Francois about our trip and he also wanted to join us but Nicole had no desire to see the poverty she expected to find in India. Reluctantly, Francois stayed behind as Anne and I set off on the road.

It was already spring when we left Paris; the trees along the broad avenues were in full bloom. It was good weather for hitchhiking and warm enough to sleep out at nights with little discomfort. We made our way south through France and spent our first night in a barn, which a farmer kindly offered for our use. We slept comfortably on the bales of hay he left for us. We then cut across northern Italy to the Adriatic and proceeded down the coast of Yugoslavia. Yugoslavia was still a communist country in those days and not well developed. In the towns dotting the coastal road, locals rented out rooms in their homes to travelers and offered meals to supplement their incomes. It was hard for Anne and me to pass up the opportunity to sleep in a warm bed and shower with hot water, so we spent a few nights on the Adriatic coast, enjoying the hospitality of the Croatians and the beauty of the Adriatic Sea.

In southern Yugoslavia we left the coast road to travel east through mountainous Montenegro on our way to northern Greece. The road through Montenegro was narrow and simply built. It wound through several miles of steep mountains dotted with villages, the people dressed in brightly colored gypsy-like outfits. The girls and women wore scarves of reds and blues and long dresses that came down to their shoes. Large groups of children appeared on the roads on their way home from school, laughing and playing, with rosy faces exuding the vibrancy of the pure mountain air. Montenegro seemed an idyllic spot for me, its people living simple lives surrounded by the beauty of nature, isolated from the urban civilization of Europe. Luckily, we found one ride that took us all the way through Montenegro, an eight-hour journey, into Macedonia and then into northern Greece.

By this time the weather had turned cold again, making sleeping outside difficult. Anne and I hitchhiked without stopping to Thessalonika, a Greek port city on the Aegean Sea and just a day's journey from Istanbul. We slept in the cars that carried us through Greece rather than risk sleeping in the cold. Once in Thessaloniki we spent a night at an inn, enjoyed a hot dinner and then breakfast, and bought some warmer clothes that would be necessary as we crossed into central Asia, where spring had not yet arrived.

We arrived in Istanbul the next day and found a hotel in the neighborhood of the historic Blue Mosque, originally a Christian church named Saint Sophia, built by the emperor Justinian the Great in the fifth century. Istanbul was large and busy, with an overwhelming amount of traffic, noise, and pollution. The city had connected the cultures of Europe and Asia for centuries and contained elements of both in an unusual mix. In those days the famous harbor of the Golden Horn on the Bosphorus was terribly polluted and the historic sections of the city were in disrepair. The political climate was highly charged, with intense antagonism between the right and left and different ethnic groups.

In Istanbul we met fellow travelers returning from the East who gave us tips on how to navigate through Turkey, Iran, and Afghanistan. We learned that the train that had run from Istanbul to Tehran was no longer in service and now stopped about two-thirds of the way through Turkey. After five nights in Istanbul, we were again ready to travel. I, for one, longed for the peace and beauty of the countryside and was glad to leave the noise and pollution of Istanbul behind.

We booked a train from Istanbul to its final stop in eastern Turkey and managed to get a cabin to ourselves. As we traveled from Istanbul, the Turks on the train grew simpler, rougher, and less tolerant of us. They did not like the idea of a Western man and woman traveling together so openly. Several times during the night ride through Anatolia, Turks banged on the door of our cabin, laughing at us and trying to provoke us. We did not rise to the bait and stayed in our cabin until we reached Ankara, where we disembarked to get away from the rowdiness.

It was a short reprieve. After we booked a room at a small hotel in Ankara, Turks knocked on our door all through the night, laughing and yelling at us until the early morning. It was highly unnerving but we did not feel physically threatened. The next day we explored Ankara, which was perched on a high, barren plateau in central Turkey, with very little in the way of greenery or trees. It seemed a cold and unwelcoming city to us and we were anxious to leave it behind. That afternoon we again boarded the train for eastern Turkey.

One more incident marred our travels. The train took us to a town in Eastern Anatolia, where we were told a bus would take us to the Iranian border. Several other Western travelers disembarked here and we all gathered at an outdoor café to have lunch and wait for the bus that would take us eastward. A group of five or six young Turks came to the café and started yelling at us and throwing stones. We outnumbered them, but this was not our territory, so we hastily grabbed our bags and made our way to the bus stop. Luckily we were not followed.

My last impression of Turkey was of crossing the high plateau of Eastern Anatolia, its stark yellow landscape bordered by chains of mountains to the north and south. The beauty and mystic quality of its vast, empty spaces deeply moved me. Finally, before reaching Iran, we saw Mount Ararat rise from the deserted plains to the north in impressive beauty. It seemed so close but it took hours before Mount Ararat was finally behind us and we could see it no more. Although some of the Turks on this trip were crude and unwelcoming, I would remember Turkey for the mystic quality of its spacious plains and rugged mountains, an untamed and rugged environment that fostered a rugged and sometimes harsh people.

The border to Iran was at a checkpoint in a mountain pass. All the bus passengers had to disembark with their baggage and pass through both Turkish and Iranian customs on foot. On the Iranian side, we were met by a jovial bus driver who sported a surprisingly modern, well-equipped bus elaborately decorated with large comfortable seats, red carpet in the aisles, and a deluxe sound system playing popular Iranian music. Where the Turks had been cold, hard, and aloof, the Iranians were warm, jovial, and welcoming, and eager to offer their services to us. The first town past the border was Maku, set in a stark valley between two high, barren, snow-covered cliffs. It was still winter in this mountainous part of western Iran and patches of snow lay on the side of the road and throughout the town. We entered late in the evening and were taken to the town's only hotel, where all of the Western travelers, men and women, slept in the same large room, in small but comfortable beds. I later discovered that many hotels in Iran and Afghanistan had such a room set up for travelers who arrived late in the night.

In the morning the hotel offered a simple breakfast and we were led to the bathhouse, or *hammam*, which was immaculate. It was an unexpected pleasure after our long days on the road. We spent the day visiting the local shops, drinking Iranian tea, and enjoying the local merchants, who were exceptionally friendly. We were told that the Iranians were Shia Muslims and most of the Iranians we met had names deriving from the first leaders of the Shia movement.

I felt a close karmic connection to Iran and Maku was a stunning introduction to the country, due to the friendliness of its people and its starkly beautiful setting. The melodious sound of the Parsi language also made a deep impression on me, so different from the harsher sounds of the Arabic and Turkish languages. Parsi, I later learned, was the tongue of some of the world's greatest spiritual poets: Rumi, Hafiz, and Sanai. It was a language of sweet sounds that reminded me of softly flowing water.

By this time about eight Westerners were in our group and we decided to travel together through Iran and Afghanistan. This company offered Anne and me a certain sense of security we had not felt in Turkey. We traveled slowly across eastern Iran, making our way from the mountains to the high plains, the solitary road cutting through sparsely populated farmlands and villages. The feeling of Iran was distinctly different from that of Turkey. Where Turkey was rough, poor, and sometimes crude, the Iranian culture had a feeling of refinement and antiquity, although Iranians also lived very simply in these rural settings. We passed through Shiraz and Tabriz and finally arrived in Tehran, the capital and Iran's largest city.

Tehran was mysteriously quiet and subdued for such a large city. I was not sure why. Still, the people were welcoming, if restrained. We explored for a few days and spent a lot of time walking to balance our many days sitting in buses and trains. After a few days, missing the clean air and quiet of the countryside, we boarded another bus to the city of Mashhad in northwestern Iran, near the Afghan border. The long journey was beginning to wear on us; we had not had the opportunity to stop and settle in one place since we started our trip. Also, our meals were erratic and we occasionally came down with dysentery. Anne and I both hoped that we would soon be able to spend a more prolonged period in a place that was both interesting and welcoming. On our first night in Mashhad, we found a restaurant where a musician sat on a stage and played haunting melodies on a violin-like instrument called a *kamancheh*. The music had a profound mystical quality that seemed strangely familiar and resonated deep within me. It reminded me how important music was to me, how, without words, it was able to open up vast domains of feeling in me. I knew instinctively that this music had a spiritual source. Mashad had been the home of several Sufi orders and I wondered if this musician was a Sufi.

After two days in Mashhad, we were back on a bus headed for the Afghan border. I had been surprised at the abrupt change we experienced when we crossed into Iran from Turkey. Entering Afghanistan, we were again introduced to a culture and landscape sharply distinct from the one we had just left. To an American, Iran was a simple but clean country, one with a strong culture and ancient tradition that was recognizable everywhere—in its music, art, architecture, and language. The culture of Afghanistan was that of the frontier, a rough and tribal culture tied closely to the mountains and valleys of the land. It was vital and simple, yet welcoming in a way we had not yet experienced in Central Asia.

The first town across the border was Herat, an ancient town first built by Alexander the Great over two thousand years ago. Some of the original structures still remained. Herat was a lively, dusty town, perched on the Afghan plateau, with a broad, unpaved, main street from which other dusty, brown streets wound into the core of the city. None of the buildings, except its impressive mosque, exceeded two stories. Our hotel offered a simple room with a stone floor covered by a simple carpet, with no furniture at all. One window opened to the main street below. A ledge about a meter wide ran the length of the far wall. It was not much but for Anne and me it was our first home in several weeks. The Afghans were friendly and accommodating. It was easy to have tea or a simple meal sent to our room from the local shops. Next door a baker made fresh naan, a delicious, large, flatbread, in ovens dug deeply into the ground.

Many Afghans rode horses, giving the town a frontier feeling. Several hotels had been set up to house the small but steady flow of young Western travelers now making the overland trek from Europe to India. The Afghans and Westerners got along well, as the Afghans felt the true interest and respect many of the Westerners held for the Afghan culture and way of life. Anne and I spent two weeks in Herat exploring the city and spending some needed quiet time together. One day we wandered into a courtyard where a crowd of people surrounded a boy who was lying on the ground. As we got closer, I saw that the boy was writhing with a beatific expression on his face, making sounds I could not understand. It dawned on me that he was speaking in tongues and that the Afghans surrounding him were familiar with and marveling at his experience. It was another reminder to me of the vast spiritual dimension hidden in the West, yet recognized and accepted in this simple culture of Afghanistan.

It was spring in Herat, and the daily presence of the sun was a welcome relief from the cold and austere climate we experienced in Turkey and Iran. At this point in our trip, Anne and I realized that we did not have enough funds to make it to India. The thought of entering India with little or no money did not bother me at the time but it was too much for Anne. Also, by this time in our journey, I sensed that for my trip to India to be a true spiritual pilgrimage, it would be better for me to do it alone. So, we traveled to Kandahar and Kabul and then took the same route back to Paris.

At the time two roads traversed Afghanistan: one to the north, which lead to the town of Mazar-i-Sharif and then down to Kabul, and one to the south, which lead to Kandahar and then up to Kabul. An unpaved horse trail also cut through the mountains of central Afghanistan. It was supposedly beautiful but dangerous. We chose the road to the south and planned to spend a few days in both Kandahar and Kabul before returning to Herat.

Kabul was a relatively small town at the time and its hotel district for foreigners spread only a few square blocks. The hotels were simple but normally built to surround a garden or courtyard, creating an atmosphere of space and being close to nature. Our hotel contained a restaurant, where each evening an Afghan musician sang and played the *rubab*, a stringed instrument with a drone-like quality like a sitar. Again the music took me to a deep place within and spoke to me intimately of the culture of Afghanistan and its deep spiritual roots.

On returning to Herat, we were able to rent our previous hotel room, which now seemed like a home. We soon found a British man named Pete who owned a small, well-appointed bus he regularly drove back and forth between London and Delhi with a busload of Westerners. He was on his way to Istanbul and had some open seats. It would take ten days to drive directly from Herat to Istanbul and he charged us twenty dollars apiece. It was a deal we could not pass up. Pete was spending about a week in Herat before taking off and we welcomed the prospect of another week in Herat before hitting the road again.

A few days before our scheduled departure, Anne and I were strolling through Herat and walked into a tall Frenchman with wild red hair—Francois! He was so disappointed about not accompanying us on our trip that, after several days, he set out alone hoping to find us before we reached India. By now Francois, Anne, and I were all close, so the three of us were elated to find ourselves together again. We spent several days exploring Herat as Anne and I showed Francois all of the haunts we had found.

The bus trip back across Iran and Turkey was arduous but joyful. The bus was filled with an adventurous crew of Westerners who had been traveling in India and Afghanistan. Two brothers, who grew up on a farm in central France, had explored the rugged mountains of the Hindu Kush in northern Afghanistan. A young German man with a drug problem had spent months in India during which he developed a deep relationship with Christ. A group of Americans were returning from three months at an ashram in western India. It was an exiting group; the ten-hour days on the bus passed quickly as we traded stories of our journeys and shared our lives. In Tehran our bus was stopped by police who wanted to check for drugs but when they entered the bus, they only casually glanced around and did little, if any, searching. Pete, our British bus driver, seemed knowledgeable of the local police and also knew the best hotels and restaurants for us along the way. We were well taken care of on our ten-day journey.

Shortly before reaching the border of Iran and Turkey, one of the men on the bus confided that he had bought two large slabs of hashish in Afghanistan that he planned to smuggle across the border and sell in Europe. Anne and I pleaded with him not to cross the Turkish border with the hashish. Already many stories were circulating of Americans caught in Turkey for possession of hashish and languishing in sordid jails for years. We did not want him to risk it. But the man was adamant and did not change his mind until we were almost to the border. Finally, he chucked the drugs in a garbage bin before we reached the border, where the Turks inspected every inch of the bus. It was a close call. The Turks did not search his body, where he had intended to hide the hash, but they did search everyone's bags and even dismantled parts of the bus where drugs could have been concealed.

After ten days on the road, we finally reached Istanbul. Anne and I no longer had enough funds to pay for a ride to Paris on the

Orient Express, so the three of us hitched a ride out of Istanbul with a German man in a Volkswagen bug. We rode with him all the way to Strasbourg, France, just across from the German border. Anne and I stayed in Strasbourg for a few days to tour the city, while Francois, missing Nicole, took a train back to Paris. Finally, Anne and I landed back in Paris, our journey ended, and we considered how to proceed next.

Since Anne was no longer an au pair, she returned home to California to finish her college studies. I still wanted to go to India but could not do so until I earned enough money to take me there and back, so I too decided to return to the U.S., to New York, where I had a friend who was a construction contractor. I knew he would have work for me. So in that early summer of 1972, Anne flew to California and I to New York, ending our journey through Europe and Central Asia.

Chapter 6

INDIA

It was hot in New York that summer of 1972. My friend Duck was working as a contractor fixing up apartments in Manhattan. He needed help putting up sheetrock, sanding, plastering, and with all the unskilled, dirty work untrained construction workers do. We worked sixteen-hour days together and made a lot of money in a couple of months. I slept on the floor of Duck's apartment. By the end of August, I had what I thought was enough money to fly back to Paris, hitchhike again to Istanbul, take trains and buses again across Central Asia to India, and then do the trip in reverse. I was wrong but it did not keep me from flying back to Paris in August to start my journey to India.

I spoke to Anne quite a few times by phone. She was re-enrolling at Berkeley and wanted to finish her degree. I wanted to visit her before leaving for Europe but did not want to risk traveling through Europe and Asia in the cold weather. So I promised I would see her in California when I returned from India. I now felt it was best for me to make the spiritual journey alone.

When I arrived in Paris, I found Francois and Nicole housesitting a large apartment on the Rue Mouffetard, a stylish and hip street in the Latin Quarter. Two days after I arrived, they both left Paris for several weeks to vacation with Nicole's parents, so I was left with a beautiful apartment to myself. I was not alone for long. Within a few days, the apartment was full of fellow travelers from America and Europe who greatly appreciated a beautiful place to crash in the heart of the Latin Quarter. After two weeks I was having so much fun that India slipped my mind. Then one night a group of us were sitting in the living room, laughing and talking. I decided to do some hatha yoga, which I had been doing daily throughout my days on the road. I started my routine by doing a headstand. As I was holding the posture, a vision of India suddenly appeared in my mind. It was so vivid that I knew it was a message for me to start my trip quickly or I would not make it out of Paris.

The next day I checked the bulletin board outside Shakespeare and Company for rides out of Paris and found a note by a young Serbian woman seeking a partner to hitchhike to Yugoslavia. I looked her up that afternoon and early the next morning we were hitchhiking out of Paris. It was always easier hitchhiking with a woman. We traveled the same route I had been on with Anne just a few months before, through France, across northern Italy, over to Trieste, and then down the Dalmatian coast of Yugoslavia. At one point our paths diverged and she headed east to Belgrade, while I continued south along the coast road. Alone at last, my journey took on an altogether different feel. I was carrying spiritual books to read in the evenings when I was alone and on the long train and bus rides across Asia. One of the books was Ouspensky's *In Search of the Miraculous,* the story of the remarkable work he did under the guidance of the spiritual master G. I. Gurdjieff in early twentieth-century Russia.

It was late summer when I reached Istanbul and the weather was mild. I had no desire to spend time in this cacophonous, polluted city. Within a day I booked a train to eastern Turkey. This time, traveling alone without a Western woman, no one bothered me or gave me much notice. I made good time and did not stop until the train line ended in eastern Anatolia, where I took buses to the Iranian border. Again I met up with several Western travelers en route and we traveled as a group through the rest of Turkey, through Iran, and into Afghanistan. Flowers and trees bloomed on sparse landscapes that months before I could not imagine would support anything so delicate or beautiful. Melons were being harvested all through eastern Turkey, Iran, and Afghanistan, a welcome addition to the simple meals we took on the road.

I made great haste to reach India before the colder weather beset Central Asia. The longest I spent in one place was one night until we reached Herat. I rented the same hotel room that had been a home away from home for Anne and me and stayed there a week, trying to get my legs back after the long days on the road. Finally, I took off for Kabul, the farthest east I had traveled before with Anne, with growing excitement that everything after would be unknown territory. Kabul was located on the far eastern corner of the high Afghan plateau that gave Afghanistan its arid and cool environment. The city itself resembled a moonscape, with a mass of one-story dwellings sitting on a barren plain flanked by the high mountain ranges of the Hindu Kush to the north. I spent a few days in Kabul but was anxious to move on. I ended up taking a minibus from Kabul through the eastern Afghan town of Jalalabad and then down the Khyber Pass to Pakistan. The terrain rapidly changed as we descended the pass, the climate becoming warmer and more humid until, when we reached Pakistan, it was unbelievably hot and damp. Where the weather in Afghanistan had been pleasantly cool and dry, it was now monsoon time in Pakistan and the roads were covered with mud. Flies swarmed everywhere and there was little escape from the stifling heat.

I spent a few days in the old hill station of Peshawar, then a quaint town in the hills of western Pakistan at the far northwestern border of old British India. Next, a series of mini-buses took me across Pakistan to the border town Lahore, where I hoped to quickly pass into India. Pakistan had just lost a war to India and the morale of the people was low. I had never seen such squalor and poverty and was hoping India would not be as bad. Unfortunately, the border between Pakistan and India was only open once a week due to the war and I was forced to spend a week in Lahore in a seedy hotel. The food was exceptionally bad and by the time I was finally able to cross the border, I had a mild but aggravating case of dysentery.

I had to cross the border between Pakistan and India on foot before I could board another bus in India. Again, crossing the border was like entering a new world. The Indian state of Punjab, which borders Pakistan at Lahore, is the green, fertile breadbasket of India. Once within Indian Punjab, there were green fields of rice and villages stretching out as far as the eye could see. Although hot and humid from the monsoon rains, the Punjab was simply beautiful and infinitely cleaner and more orderly than what I had seen in Pakistan. My heart leapt in my chest with excitement. I was finally in India. I had a deep feeling that I had come home.

Not knowing where to go first, I took a bus to the Golden Temple in Amritsar, the spiritual home of the Sikhs and the Indian town nearest the border. The Golden Temple is an ancient structure, considered the holiest site in the Sikh religion. At that time the Sikhs allowed pilgrims and travelers to stay in rooms within the temple for a minimal fee. The main steps into the temple were guarded by two tall, thin, very old but impressive-looking Sikhs wearing only *lungis*, a piece of cloth tied across their waists. Their hair and beards were long and white. They carried long tridents I imagined were symbols of their protection of the holy shrine. The suffocating crowd of pilgrims and tourists, along with the unfamiliar heat and humidity, created an oppressive atmosphere for me. I spent a night in a room filled with Sikh pilgrims, the lone overhead fan barely moving the stagnant air. The next morning, consulting my map of

India, I decided to immediately head north toward the mountains to escape the brutal heat. Being on the far western border of India, the nearest mountainous destination that attracted me was Dharamsala, in the northern state of Himachal Pradesh, where Tibetan refugees had set up their government in exile under the Dalai Lama.

Again I set out, taking buses from one town to the next on roads barely paved and rutted with mud. The rains continued. I stayed in hotels in tiny rooms where little air circulated, even with ceiling fans humming above, and ate spicy Indian meals at local restaurants. My dysentery, although not severe, continued. Finally, I reached the town of Pathankot, where the road began to climb into the foothills that preceded the Himalayas. As we slowly ascended the mountains, the air became cooler and fresher and I felt my mood lift. After several hours on the road, we stopped at a tea shop in a small town on the mountain road. I looked out over the vast, sweltering plains of India below me and felt gratitude that I would not have to bear the heat, noise, and squalor of those plains another day. The towns we passed on the mountain road were also poor and simple but it was a simplicity pleasant to the senses and spirit. Slowly we ascended until we neared Dharamsala, at over nine thousand feet. Now the plains were far below us and the crisp, clear, pine-scented mountain air washed away all my memories of the heat and smells of the plains.

The village where the Dalai Lama resided, called McLeod Ganj, was a bit farther up the mountain from the main part of Dharamsala and I decided this was to be my destination. There I found a community of Tibetans with their own unique culture. Surprisingly, there was little evidence of anything Indian in Dharamsala. The town at that time was extremely simple and small and built almost entirely within feet of the narrow, winding road that led up the mountain. Very little was flat in this town other than its short main street. Everywhere I looked were spectacular views of the mountains descending below us. On the main street were a few Tibetan hotels, where I noticed several young Westerners. In the middle of the street was a large square filled with colorful Tibetan prayer flags and prayer wheels, in use day and night. Many Tibetan dwellings of mud and brick lined the road past the main section of the village. I booked a room in the largest hotel in town, a two-story building overlooking the main square. There were other Westerners staying there and, after settling in my room, I sought them out.

One of the first things I noticed about the Westerners in Dharamsala was a look of serenity and contentment I was not used to seeing in fellow travelers on the road. They did not have the beaten-down, tired look many travelers had in India from the heat, traveling conditions, and difficulty in finding good food. Most of them had come to study Buddhist Dharma from the Tibetan lamas who resided with the Dalai Lama. A two-story school had been built farther up the mountain, which held classrooms and meditation rooms, and many of the Westerners were actively engaged in studying Buddhism there. There were also Westerners like me who considered themselves spiritual seekers but who were at this point more observers than practitioners. I met no Westerners in Dharamsala who were not drawn there to satisfy some spiritual longing.

Dharmasala was pervaded by an elevated and peaceful energy I later learned comes from the presence of people sincerely committed to their spiritual growth and their daily observance of spiritual practices. At the time I was sensitive to this energy but unaware of its source or significance. I also found that this energy made it uncomfortable for me when negative thoughts or feelings came up. Added to the spiritual atmosphere was the purity and beauty of the high mountainous setting that cradled this small town and instilled deep wonder in me wherever I looked. It was monsoon season in Dharamsala but, unlike on the plains, here the rains seemed to purify the land. There were no muddy roads caused by standing water. Here the water flowed downward through the hills and the air remained cool and fresh. Every day I looked down from my hotel room window onto the massive, dark clouds that brought the daily rains, silhouetted against the mountain cliffs. The rainy skies took on fantastic shades of blues and reds in their interplay with the sun and mountains, all heightening my sense of wonder and beauty.

My close relationships with some of the Westerners in Dharamsala made my time there interesting and enjoyable. I was curious and asked many questions. I wanted to know how practicing Buddhism had changed these people and what they had gained from it. I was advised by many to join a course on Buddhist Dharma given by a Tibetan lama at the new school. One morning I trekked up the narrow mountain path to the school and sat in on a lecture by thDhondene lama, whose teachings were translated into English by a young Canadian man. The discourse was about the mind and mental perceptions but, being unfamiliar with the terms and concepts, I could understand little of what he taught and left the session more confused than inspired.

Although not drawn to the Buddhist teachings, I felt at home in Dharamsala and felt a natural sense of reverence and respect for the many Buddhist monks and nuns I encountered there. Many exhibited a quality of natural and unforced friendliness and kindness I had rarely witnessed before. I was drawn to their sense of compassion and single-minded commitment to their spirituality, as I had been drawn to Lanza del Vasto's dedication to his spiritual path.

During my stay in Dharamsala, my dysentery progressively worsened and I told this to the Canadian translator. He took me to see the Dalai Lama's physician, Yeshi Donden, a famous practitioner of traditional Tibetan medicine, who diagnosed me by taking my pulse in several places on my arm, all the time smiling at me reassuringly. Yeshi Donden told me my dysentery was caused by food poisoning in Pakistan from eating with wooden utensils not properly cleaned. He gave me a packet of round pills he said contained tiny amounts of gold and silver and told me to take one whenever I had symptoms of dysentery. I immediately returned to my hotel room, took one of the pills, and lay on my bed to relax. Within twenty minutes I felt a deep rumbling in my intestines, which had been irritated and distended, and saw a shaft of white light come from above and penetrate directly into my abdomen. This lasted for several minutes. When it passed, my stomach felt normal again—no pain, no dysentery, no distention. I was intensely relieved and wondered if this healing had come from the pills or from Yeshi Donden.

I spent two weeks in Dharamsala before deciding to explore other parts of India. Although I was impressed by the Tibetan Buddhist monks and the sincere Western seekers studying Buddhism, it was the Indian spiritual tradition Lanza's writings had exposed me to that had drawn me to India. I still felt a deep inner desire to discover it. On my last night in Dharamsala, a group of about fifteen Westerners gave me a going-away party in one of the large dormitory rooms at the hotel. There was a guitar available and for a few hours I played while we all sang songs from the 60s. A Tibetan man also played guitar and I showed him some chords to the songs so we could play together. There was a lot of love in that group and for a moment I pictured myself staying in Dharamsala. It was so comforting to share that type of friendship. I knew I'd be on the road alone again the next day and it was not easy to find such sympathetic companions. Nonetheless, I was determined to pursue what India had to offer and the next morning I was on a bus to Delhi.

I did not have a plan when I left for Delhi. It was a long bus ride and the descent to the plains brought back the heat and smells of India that had greeted me when I first arrived. This time I was better able to deal with it. Delhi itself held no attraction for me, so once there I headed south. I had heard about the beautiful, untouched beaches of Goa and, after so many weeks of traveling, relished the opportunity for ocean swimming and long hikes on secluded beaches. My body desperately needed some rejuvenating exercise. I also read of a town in southern India near Goa called Hampi that had many temples where sadhus congregated during the monsoon. Images from Lanza del Vasto's book of Indian holy men traveling from temple to temple on foot had made a deep impression on me and I resolved to attempt to experience this myself.

After a few days in Delhi, I booked a third-class train to Mumbai. It happened to be a mail train and stopped in virtually every village along the way. The Indian train system allowed sadhus to travel freely by third-class and I wanted to meet some of them on this trip but I learned the hard way that third-class train travel was painstakingly slow, hot, dirty, and uncomfortable. It took over twenty-four hours to reach Mumbai as we stopped in innumerable villages. The train lacked air conditioning or fans. The dust of the Indian plains wafted through the open windows and became caked on my skin and the smell of spicy Indian food permeated everything. Although there were several sadhus on the train, they were culturally so different than I and spoke so little English that I was able to learn very little about them.

I arrived in Mumbai at Victoria Station and took a horse-driven taxi to the docks, where I sought passage on a ship to south India. I had not slept in the past thirty-six hours. There was a boat leaving shortly for Goa. I quickly purchased a ticket for deck class and made my way to the boat only minutes before it departed. It was a three-story vessel, the bottom deck carrying poor Indians who brought their food and their belongings with them. It was crowded, hot, and smelly, not unlike the third-class train I had just taken. The second deck had far fewer passengers and had a simple restaurant and benches to sit on. Although passengers there also slept on the ground on bedrolls, it was infinitely cleaner and more spacious than the lower deck. The third deck was another world altogether, with clean whitewashed cabins and comfortable chaise lounges outside the cabins overlooking the beautiful Arabian Sea. I had purchased a deck-class ticket but since I was a Westerner, no one paid any attention to me as I spent most of the remaining daylight hours on the second deck. After dinner I climbed to the top deck to see what it was like and found it completely empty. I slept that night on a chaise lounge on the top deck. It was the most luxury I was to experience for a long time.

The next morning we arrived at Panjim harbor in Goa, where I disembarked and headed toward Anjuna, one of Goa's long pristine beaches. Goa had not yet been developed into an international tourist spot and the large luxury hotels had not yet invaded its untouched beaches. It was nearing the end of the monsoon season in Goa and the fields were thick with vibrantly green rice paddies bordered by lush rainforests. The land here was of red clay, giving the forest grounds and roads a deep reddish hue that offered a beautiful contrast to the green of the fields. Everything was acutely alive from the monsoon rains and I basked in the tropical beauty and simplicity of the environment.

I rented a room in a guest house near the beach and spent the next two weeks swimming in the churning ocean and taking long hikes along the beaches, empty except for the occasional fishermen going out in their small wooden vessels. The monsoon rains had left the ocean very rough, with nine and ten-foot waves, making swimming a rigorous endeavor. I had been on the road for such a long time without vigorous exercise that my body rejoiced at the long hours of swimming and hiking. After two weeks I was bronzed and feeling incredibly healthy. Although I occasionally had a bout of dysentery, my Tibetan pills quickly rid me of the worst symptoms. Several Westerners were staying in Goa and I had no lack of company.

After two weeks I was ready to start my trip inland on foot to Hampi. I left most of my belongings with an older Indian man I had met in Anjuna and took off on the road toward Hampi. I caught a ride, which took me about thirty kilometers out from Panjim, and then started walking, intending to sleep in temples in the villages on my way. I walked for a few hours before coming to a tiny village, where I asked for directions to the nearest temple. I was told in firm terms that I would not be allowed to sleep there. They said a non-Hindu could not sleep in their temple and I would not be welcomed in the Hindu temples on the road to Hampi. I was surprised and disheartened. On the other hand, I had begun wondering if I was crazy to sleep out in the open in the intimidating Indian heat and humidity. I re-evaluated my plans and, with some reluctance, turned back toward Panjim. Late that evening I returned to Anjuna Beach.

Back in Anjuna I realized that I was never going to live like an Indian sadhu. Lanza had done it in the 40s, but this was 1972 and I was a young, Jewish American from a privileged background, compared to how people lived in India. Moreover, I was a hippie. I liked wearing my blue jeans and tennis shoes and did not want to trade them in for a lungi and water bowl. I decided to return to the Himalayas, where I initially hoped I would find the answers to my seeking. So accustomed was I now to traveling long distances that the prospect of another thousand-mile trip did not daunt me at all. My vitality restored, I set off for the holy town of Rishikesh in the Himalayan foothills, on the sacred river Ganges. I knew Rishikesh was a place of pilgrimage where countless yogis, sadhus, and holy men flocked to its many ashrams, the Ganges, and the majestic Himalayas.

I retraced my path out of Goa by taking a boat back to Mumbai and then traveled on a second-class train to Delhi. From there I took buses into the foothills of the Himalayas, following the course of the Ganges, passing through the pilgrimage town of Haridwar and finally arriving in Rishikesh late one afternoon. The Indian buses were crude affairs lacking air conditioning and shock absorbers. The five-hour ride from Delhi left me covered with sweat and dust, my body sore from the bus' lurching across heavily rutted roads. Nonetheless, it was a great feeling to approach the mountains again and a relief to find the air cooler and the towns a bit cleaner. On the bus ride I sat next to a sadhu with the features of a south Indian, a man who seemed in his late twenties and appeared peaceful, clean, and composed. I attempted some conversation with him but he spoke no English.

Sitting next to this sadhu on the ride to Rishikesh, I read a book called *My Master* by Swami Vivekananda about the life of Sri Ramakrishna, a holy man and enlightened master who lived in Calcutta at the end of the nineteenth century. The story of

Ramakrishna's life was the first account I had read of an individual devoting his life to God realization. I had always framed my spiritual pursuit as a search for Truth and did not really know if I believed in a God. But reading the story of Ramakrishna awoke in me a deep yearning for a purity of heart and purity of love I imagined would be called God. For the first time, I could honestly say to myself I sincerely wanted to know God.

With thoughts of Ramakrishna playing through my mind, I arrived at Rishikesh, a sprawling town on the Ganges, cradled in the Himalayan foothills, which to me seemed more like mountains. It was a major pilgrimage destination for Hindus and sometimes held as many as a million pilgrims. I had arrived at a quiet time but thousands of pilgrims were there visiting the holy sites. There were many ashrams in Rishikesh and across the river in Lakshman Jhula. I managed to find accommodations outside of the Sivananda ashram in a hostel called the Swiss Cottages. Swami Sivananda had been a famous spiritual teacher in India and had set up his ashram in Rishikesh many years before. He was considered an enlightened being and had many disciples who themselves became well-known spiritual teachers in the West. He died several years before my visit but his ashram was still a major pilgrimage destination for Indian and Western seekers.

The Swiss Cottages were a few hundred yards outside the ashram and consisted of whitewashed brick cottages and a simple thatched hut. I rented the thatched hut for a rupee per day, less than twenty cents. It was immaculately clean but held nothing in it whatsoever. That did not bother me, as I was fine with my sleeping bag. One of the cottages had been rented to a tall American jazz musician named Eddie, who had been living in India for several years. He was known by Westerners traveling through India because he often provided travelers with meals, a place to stay, and lively spiritual discussions. He was called Eight-Fingered Eddie by some because of two missing fingers on one of his hands. My hut was less than a hundred yards from the Ganges and that evening, my first in

Rishikesh, I took my first swim in the sacred river. The Indian pilgrims did not swim in the Ganges; rather they bathed, fully clothed, as a ritual observance. Since I was downriver from the ashrams and bathing ghats, I was alone in a secluded spot on the river. I dove wholeheartedly into its cool depths, swimming into the current and enjoying the river's freshness and vigorous current. I spent about thirty minutes swimming before I returned to my hut, thoroughly refreshed and cleansed. The sun was setting and I needed to change my clothes and find a place to have dinner. Entering my hut, I lay down for a few moments on my sleeping bag and began to feel a fever overtake me. My body became hot and then cold, so I climbed into my sleeping bag, determined to sweat out the fever. Before long I realized that this was not an ordinary fever. Events from my past began to appear before me vividly and, for nearly twenty-four hours, I watched my life parade before me. I suspected that my dip in the Ganges was somehow bringing my karmas to the surface and hopefully purifying them.

After lying in my hut for nearly a day, the visions of my past and my fever receded. I was hungry and walked to Eddie's hut to tell him about my experience. Eddie loved talking about spiritual matters and invited me in, shared his dinner with me, and listened attentively as I described my first plunge into the Ganges. Eddie agreed that I was a beneficiary of the Ganges' healing power.

In Rishikesh I came to the conclusion that it was time for me to look for a guru, a spiritual teacher, recognizing that my attempts to teach myself spirituality and learn solely from books had not gotten me very far. I discussed this with Eddie and he laughed at the notion that anyone needed a guru. I was not so sure. I began a search of the ashrams located on the Lakshman Jhula side of the river. The first I visited was just off the Ganges and consisted of a large meditation hall and a series of block-like cottages surrounding it. I saw a swami—a monk dressed in ochre robes—in the hall and approached him to ask if there were any programs or courses where I could learn about yoga. I was wearing blue jeans and a tee shirt and sported long brown hair down to my shoulders, with a brown curly beard. My appearance evidently did not make this swami happy and he looked at me with contempt. There were no programs for people like me at his ashram, he assured me. I was amazed at his intolerance and inability to see through superficial appearances. I had a good laugh with Eddie later when I shared my experience.

At the Swiss Cottages, another swami came daily to give talks on yoga and Indian spirituality. He looked like a traditional Indian sadhu, in ochre robes, with long hair and a beard. He spoke in sugary tones about oneness and the universe being composed of nothing but bliss. I did not doubt his teachings, but I wanted to go more deeply into how one experiences this oneness and bliss. One morning I sat in on one of his talks. I asked some questions and told him that I disagreed with some of his statements. This irritated him; he angrily told me I was interrupting his teachings and asked me to leave. Amazed at the ferocity of his displeasure, I again discussed this with Eddie, who laughingly told me that this swami had a great need to teach others and be seen as a spiritual teacher.

A few days later, I came upon a small ashram in the hills above the Ganges, on the Laxman Jhula side of the river. It was a simple but beautiful setting, run by a young-looking yogi named Swami Premvarni. About ten Westerners lived at his ashram and he guided them through daily sessions of meditation, yoga, and talks about Indian spirituality. On our first meeting, he welcomed me and invited me to stay for meditation and a question/answer session. I was impressed by the Westerners there; they were clearly serious seekers intent on learning from this swami. Two of the Westerners, Durga and Kalyani, were Australian women who had been living at this ashram for a year. They took it upon themselves to explain the workings of the ashram and Swami Premvarni to me. At the end of the session, I asked the swami if I could stay there and study under him. He replied that I was not yet ready to live at his ashram but that I could come every morning at 10:00 a.m. and water the garden as a means of service and then attend his morning meditation and yoga sessions. I agreed.

For the next two weeks, I diligently woke up early, bathed in the Ganges, had breakfast at a chai shop, and then made my way up to Swami Premvarni's ashram, where I watered the garden for a half hour and then sat in on his sessions. As in Dharamsala, I enjoyed the elevated feeling of the ashram but was still unable to relate to the teachings of yoga that came from the swami. In one session he asked me to explain the difference between subjectivity and objectivity. While I was attempting my explanation, he began making faces at me as if my words were nonsense. I knew he was indicating that my understanding was purely mental and that I had to have a deeper inner experience but I was clueless about how to have this deeper experience.

The next day, a bit discouraged, I came late to the ashram. Swami Premvarni was furious with me. How could I be serious about learning from him if I could not keep the simple discipline of coming by 10:00 a.m. to water the garden? He yelled at me to get out. I was beside myself with shame. When he saw that I was taking his rejection so hard, he softened his words and told me that I was not ready yet, but when I thought I was I could come back to him and try again. I spoke to Durga and Kalyani before I left and they told me that the swami recognized I was a sincere seeker and that was why he treated me so harshly. They said the more sincere the seeker, the harder he was on them and he was just trying to make my commitment to learning stronger so I could receive his teachings. I greatly appreciated their words and left the ashram feeling better. However, I knew I would not be returning to Swami Premvarni, not because of his harsh words, but because nothing special was stirred in my heart by his teachings or his presence. I instinctively knew that what he had to offer would not be enough to satisfy my deep spiritual longings. Again my mind went back to Sri Ramakrishna, who manifested a burning hunger for God that radiated from him and infected all of his disciples, and I wondered if such a spiritual teacher still existed in India.

Having been dismissed by Swami Premvarni, I decided to travel higher into the Himalayas, where I was told many yogis still lived, but in more remote and inaccessible abodes. A fellow traveler I met in Rishikesh told me of an ashram higher in the Himalayas in a beautiful setting where a Western traveler like myself would be welcome to stay. The ashram was called Sat Tal and was located just north of the town of Nainital in the state of Uttar Pradesh, set in the mountains amid seven lakes. Before leaving I visited a local bookstore where I bought a series of four books on yoga by Ramakrishna's disciple Swami Vivekananda and determined that they would be my next reading material. Unfortunately there was no direct bus line from Rishikesh to Nainital so I was forced to take a bus south all the way to Delhi and then another from Delhi to Nainital. It was a lot of traveling but I made it to Nainital by the end of the day.

Nainital was a beautiful town set on a large lake in a valley surrounded by the Himalayan mountains. I found that my destination—Sat Tal—was even farther north, near the village of Bhuwali, and the next morning I took an early bus to this tiny town. The Sat Tal ashram was still seven miles from Bhuwali and there was no bus service there so I took to the road and started walking, hoping to catch a ride along the way. After an hour of walking, I did receive a ride to the narrow, unpaved road that led off the highway to Sat Tal. Again I walked for an hour until I reached the main buildings of the ashram.

To my surprise, Sat Tal was a Christian ashram founded by an American missionary several years before and now managed by an elderly American woman named Evelyn. Although it was Christian, the ashram was open to people of all religions who were free to engage in their own spiritual endeavors, even if not Christian. The ashram was set on a large track of mountainous land that included seven lakes and held several bungalows where visitors could stay. For five rupees a day—about one American dollar—I received a room in a bungalow, three meals per day served in the main building, and tea and biscuits at 4:00 p.m. There was no electricity or running water in the bungalow, a simple two-story wooden structure tastefully furnished with a bed, dresser, desk, and oil lamp. I bathed each morning under a tap outside the bungalow, wearing shorts Indian-style since Indians did not bathe completely naked. My room was on the second floor. Large monkeys with gray beards climbed the nearby trees to scamper on the bungalow roof.

It was now October. Those trees with leaves were turning colors and the nights were becoming cool. For the first time in India, I wore a sweater in the evenings. Few people lived at Sat Tal at this time other than Evelyn and her staff of Indian workers, who did the cooking and maintenance work. There was an elderly Indian couple who were Christian, a young American woman, and two young European men. I learned later that another American man was living in his own cottage on a more remote part of the ashram grounds. He prepared his own meals there, not partaking of the ashram meals with the other guests.

My days were spent exploring the mountainous region of this remote part of India, swimming in Sat Tal's large but cold lakes, and reading the books on yoga by Swami Vivekananda. The mountains had a mystical quality similar to what I had experienced in Dharamsala. I later realized that this was due to the many yogis who had lived in these mountains for years, doing their spiritual practices in caves and remote forest settings, lending a distinct spiritual vibration to a region where the power and beauty of nature was already strong.

I made frequent trips into the village of Bhuwali, where I picked up supplies and met other Westerners traveling in that area. Only seven miles from Bhuwali was the ashram of Neem Karoli Baba, a famous Indian holy man who attracted a number of Western followers, including the American spiritual teacher Ram Dass, who was well known among Western spiritual seekers. Talking with many of Neem Karoli's followers, I was convinced that he was indeed an enlightened teacher but I was put off by the scene of so many Western hippies congregating around him. My thinking at the time was that a spiritual path was a serious matter and I could not reconcile this with the party-like atmosphere I perceived from Neem Karoli's devotees. My perception kept me from meeting this great saint and remarkable yogi. It seems that my destiny pulled me irrevocably elsewhere.

After a few days at Sat Tal, I met Richard, the American living in the cottage farther from the bungalows where most of the ashram guests stayed. Richard was from California and had been at Sat Tal for a year, studying Sanskrit and Indian philosophy as part of a master's degree program. He had learned to speak Hindi fluently during his year in India and had also mastered Indian cooking, preparing all of his meals in his cottage in the traditional Indian way; he cooked his own rice, dal, vegetable curries, and *chapatis*— rounded flatbread—on an open fire in his cottage, then washed his utensils with ash from the fire. I was impressed. Richard also met daily with an Indian sadhu who instructed him in Indian philosophy and meditation.

Richard and I became good friends because of our shared interests. Many evenings I skipped the ashram meal and went to Richard's, where he prepared dinner and we discussed our spiritual seeking and our exposure to Indian thought. He also had a guitar, something I greatly missed playing. Our evenings together gave me the chance to sit by the fire and play the American folk and rock songs I loved so much.

My readings of Vivekananda's books started a dramatic change in my way of thinking about myself and my world. Two concepts stood out that were revolutionary for me. One was that the essence of a human being was divine and that the means to connect with this divine consciousness was through quieting the mind rather than through more thought. This was diametrically opposed to how I had gathered knowledge in the past through reading, conversations, and intense intellectualizing. It had never occurred to me that I needed to quiet my mind to understand the higher Truth. The second concept was of karma, the teaching that no action is ever lost and that a human being always receives the fruits of his actions. I had previously despaired of being able to accomplish all my goals in life and often felt that the good and productive actions I had performed would likely have little bearing on what I would attain in my life. I had sincerely felt that much of life was governed by chance. The idea that I could shape my destiny through consistent good actions was empowering and remarkable. More than this, I knew immediately that this was true.

In our discussions at meal times with Evelyn and the ashram guests, I shared my insights on karma and yoga and spoke with respect about the Indian spiritual tradition. This offended Evelyn, a die-hard Evangelical, who tried to keep a good Christian attitude about me despite my beliefs, but still shook her head sadly when I offered my ideas on spirituality. The elder Indian couple were receptive to my ideas regardless of being Christians and were surprised when I suggested that some of the Indian mythic heroes, like Hanuman the monkey god, were real.

I spent a month at Sat Tal absorbing Vivekananda's philosophy of yoga, sharing insights with Richard and the other ashram guests and imbibing the wonderful atmosphere of the Himalayas as fall continued to progress and the weather became colder. At one point I realized that Evelyn felt uncomfortable about me remaining at Sat Tal because of my unchristian beliefs, although she was careful not to tell me so directly. I did not want to overstay my welcome or offend Evelyn, whom I had grown to like and appreciate for her tolerance of my ideas. So I decided to leave Sat Tal and travel higher into the Himalayas to the town of Almora, near the Nepalese border, where the Western Buddhist teacher Lama Govinda had resided for years.

Again I traveled by bus through the mountain roads to Almora, a five-hour trip through towns and villages, until I arrived at this hill station perched in the Himalayas. Almora was a small, busy town. I quickly discovered that the Westerners who traveled there stayed about three miles up the mountain in a little village called Kasar Devi. There was no transportation to Kasar Devi so I walked the three miles up the steep mountain path. About halfway there, I met an American named Das who had been living there for some time. Das was truly a free spirit. He was younger than I, perhaps only twenty, and walked around Almora barefoot in his white lungi. For a young man a surprising wisdom and compassion radiated from him. He seemed truly at home in India. He told me of a cottage in Kasar Devi where I would be welcome to stay and have meals for a few rupees per day. Das didn't live in Kasar Devi but in a cottage about two miles up the road from Almora, where our ways parted.

As I climbed the mountain road, the scenery became breathtaking. Blue, purple, and red flowers covered the hills on each side of the road, the colors so radiant and clear that each flower seemed to subtly vibrate with its own unearthly light. At one point I climbed through the clouds into a land of high mountain peaks that towered above the clouds. At the summit, I found Kasar Devi, a village of one street with a few homes and a tea shop. I found the home Das mentioned and was greeted by a pair of Germans who rented space to fellow travelers. They also shared the meals they prepared for themselves each noon and evening for a small fee. They were both great cooks and had mastered the intricacies of Indian cooking.

I spent much of my time in Kasar Devi reading and contemplating the books on yoga by Vivekananda and exploring the mountainous area surrounding Almora. Some days I hiked the three miles to Almora in the morning and retraced my steps back up the narrow, unpaved road later in the day. As in the other Himalayan sites I had visited, Almora too was permeated with an elevated energy I was now becoming used to, having spent almost three months in these mountainous regions where many yogis still lived and performed their spiritual practices. Many of the yogis that Paramahamsa

Yogananda, author of *Autobiography of a Yogi*, had written about lived in this region and I began to recognize this spiritual vibration more and more.

Although I was greatly impressed with the wonder and beauty of Kasar Devi, I soon realized that I would not find a spiritual teacher there and decided not to remain very long. One morning, I began to plan for my departure and, walking into Almora, ran into Das. We ate lunch together at a tiny restaurant in town that served typical Indian fare with a lot of chilis and spices. It was tasty but I knew immediately on leaving the restaurant that my digestion was not right. For the past three months I had carried the packet of Tibetan medicine given me by Yeshi Donden, the Dalai Lama's physician in Dharamsala. Every time I had the slightest symptoms of dysentery, I took one of those pills and my dysentery largely disappeared. Unfortunately I had taken my last pill at Sat Tal and now had nothing to prevent another bout of dysentery.

That night I stayed in town to see the folks of Almora put on a theatrical production of the Ramlila, the life of Lord Rama. In the Hindu religion, Rama is considered an incarnation of God. His story, written in the Ramayana, is known by Indians of all ages. The play, performed and sung in Hindi, was the story of how Rama learned that his wife Sita had been kidnapped by the demon Ravana and how Rama was aided by his faithful servants, the monkey king Hanuman, and his brother Lakshmana, to overcome many obstacles and finally kill Ravana and rescue Sita. I did not understand much of what was happening in the play but the feeling as the story unfolded was electric. I also greatly enjoyed sitting outdoors under the Himalayan night sky with the people of Almora, observing how the town's children were enthralled by the story. That night, after the performance, a tea shop owner allowed Das and me to sleep on the benches in his shop so we did not have to make the trek back up the mountain.

Waking the next day, I could tell I was in trouble. My dysentery had become worse and I sorely missed the Tibetan medicine I needed to counteract it. Knowing I was not going to stay much longer in Almora, I decided to immediately depart for Delhi to find a Western doctor. I trekked back up to Kasar Devi and spent the day packing and saying my goodbyes. The next morning, I hiked back down to Almora and took a bus to Delhi. It was chilly the morning I departed, a beautiful mountain coolness I was reluctant to leave. I felt a distinct sense of loss as I gradually descended the Himalayas to the Indian plains. On the ride I could feel my stay in India coming to a close. My three-month visa was due to expire shortly and I did not think I had a chance of getting it extended by the officials in Delhi. Most Westerners who needed to extend their stay had to travel to either Pakistan or Nepal and apply for new visas to reenter. Because of my dysentery I had no desire to take such a journey. In Delhi a doctor gave me some Western medicine but it did not seem to help. A bit demoralized and weak from the dysentery, I phoned my parents in the U.S. and asked them to wire me three hundred dollars so I could fly back home. I had enough funds to return to Paris overland but was in no shape to undertake such a grueling trip again.

I stayed in Delhi for a week while I waited for the funds to arrive and arranged for my flight home. It was late November. My dysentery was now more manageable but not gone. I met a group of Westerners in Delhi who were also traveling back to the States and we all managed to get on the same flight. We stopped in London for two nights and stayed at a fellow traveler's apartment there. As expected, it was cold in London. Without a warm coat, I roamed London wrapped in my gray wool Indian blanket. I loved it. I was such a hippie.

Chapter 7

MOROCCO REVISITED

O n my return America seemed a cold and unwelcoming place. Having imbibed the high vibration of Indian spirituality, returning to the materialistic environment of the States was a shock to my system. I had been subtly changed by the lamas, yogis, and sincere fellow seekers I met in India and equally influenced by the sacred environments of the Himalayas and Ganges. Without a clue about how to continue my spiritual search in this fast-paced environment, I was simply lost.

After seeing my parents in Pennsylvania, I visited friends in Boston who were more than glad to put me up. I stayed with them for about a month and then left to visit Anne in California. I took a five-day Greyhound bus ride to Berkeley in December, right before Christmas. Anne was delighted to see me and I was surprised to find how glad I was to see her too. Our relationship picked up where we had left off in Paris. She lived in a large apartment near the Berkeley campus, which she shared with a fellow female student who also seemed happy to have me around. Through Christmas we had a great time together, sharing our familiar bond and hanging out in Berkeley.

However, in January, when Anne's classes resumed, I didn't know how to proceed. I had no desire to hang out in Berkeley while she completed her degree. I also wanted to renew my spiritual search but was unsure what my next step should be. Anne sensed my dissatisfaction and it made her uncomfortable. She was hoping that I would make a deeper commitment to our relationship but I knew I couldn't make any commitment until I resolved a more basic issue about myself: who was I anyway?

These thoughts consumed me. Although Anne could relate to them, she was more interested in pursuing a normal relationship. Reluctantly, we went our own ways. I said goodbye to Anne that January in Berkeley. The next day she drove me to the Greyhound station, where I started the five-day, mid-winter, cross-country trip back to Boston.

My friends were surprised to see me when I returned. Not knowing what else to do, I decided to try one more trip to Morocco. I had loved Morocco my first time there and it had opened my eyes to spirituality. Perhaps Morocco had more to offer me. It was surely better than living aimlessly in America. I had barely any money left so I funded my trip by selling the fine collection of books I had accumulated over the years, including many hard-to-find volumes on literature, philosophy, and political thought. My spiritual seeking had taken me to a place where I no longer cherished these books and, to my mind, no longer needed them.

In February 1973 I returned to Paris and again stayed with Francois and Nicole. I soon felt better and had a sense that my seeking would continue. I spent two months in Paris and spent more money than I should have before undertaking my trip to Morocco. Francois and Nicole were living in a new, larger apartment on the

Left Bank in a part of Paris that I dearly loved, making it hard for me to leave in those early months of spring when Paris was so beautiful.

Finally, in April, I took off for Morocco, hitchhiking again through France and Spain down to Malaga, where I was able to take a boat to the port city of Melilla on the eastern shore of Spanish Morocco, near the Algerian border. I hitchhiked through the Rif mountains that extend east-west across northern Morocco. This sparsely populated part of Morocco held only villages tucked away in remote mountain settings. On the road, I met a traveler from France, Antoine, who had traveled through Morocco several times before and intimately knew the countryside. We hitchhiked together through the Rif and then through the Atlas Mountains to southern Morocco.

In April the weather in the Rif was already warm, making traveling easy. The roads winding through the Rif were narrow and simply built, with little traffic, and offered wonderful views of the mountain vistas. We reached a village called Ketama, noted for its hashish production. Looking out from a tea shop, we viewed fields of hemp as far as the eye could see. We joked with the proprietor that Ketama left little room for growing vegetables and we wondered what they ate! On the road past Ketama, we found an old Moroccan man with beard and turban who was bathing himself in a stream that trickled down the mountain. He joyfully indicated that we should follow him down a steep, windy path leading into a narrow valley.

We followed the old man for an hour to a village in a beautiful valley that was formed by a river of sparkling water. Our host showed us his home and took us to a barn where we were to sleep on piles of hay. There were less than a dozen houses in the village and it seemed fewer than thirty people lived there, including several children. The river had a cooling effect on the village. We learned that it was the source of the village's drinking water and were careful not to compromise its purity. To wash our clothes, we carried buckets of water sufficiently away from the river so that none of our detergent went back into the it.

We spent two nights in the village. The old man was a great host and woke us both mornings with freshly-brewed cups of coffee highlighted with fragrant rose petals and fresh honey. Since the villagers spoke little French, communication was limited but their goodwill and generosity were plainly evident. We were reluctant to leave this beautiful spot and the wonderful hospitality the villagers showed us.

Following our plan, Antoine and I proceeded west through the Rif and then south through the Atlas Mountains, which run north-south through central Morocco. We continued to hitchhike and passed through many small towns and villages until we reached Fez. Several nights we were put up by Moroccan families, who offered us space in their homes and shared their food with us. In one home the two of us slept in a family bed with the husband, wife, and children. The Moroccan hospitality was warm and impeccable. Even the poorest farmer gladly shared whatever he had with a visitor.

Antoine was a French Jew whose ancestors had come from Morocco, making him intensely interested in the Moroccans and their culture. He was also a spiritual seeker with knowledge of the mystic traditions of Judaism. We had many long discussions as we made our way south through Morocco. In Fez, needing a respite from our hitchhiking, we booked a hotel for a few days. Fez was an ancient mountain town of exquisite Arabic architecture, with narrow cobbled streets, intriguing shops and restaurants, and impressive mosques. We saw wonderful artwork for sale: Arabic engravings and tiles, colorful carpets and weavings, handiwork in gold and silver, and beautiful Moroccan fabrics and clothing. It was a unique and beautiful town and we were again reluctant to leave.

We hitchhiked all the way to Essaouira, my home two years before. My previous stay in Essaouira had been in winter, with the weather rather cold. Now, in May, it was much warmer and at midday hot. Not intending to stay long, we found a hotel in which a group of Westerners had rented a large room with space for several travelers to lay out their sleeping bags. The fee was only one dirham per night, or about twenty American cents. One evening I ran into Abdulsalem as I wandered through the inner quarters. He recognized me at once and displayed great happiness to see me but I could tell from his nervous glances that he was now more involved in his underground political struggle and believed he was in danger. Our meeting was brief and I knew it best that we not meet again.

At this point Antoine decided to return to France and I headed to Marrakech, which was only a two-hour bus ride inland from Essaouira. Marrakech was an ancient Moroccan town built on a desert of red sand, surrounded by high, reddish-brown walls. Several gates led into and out of the city. The old town was surrounded by a newer, more modern French city, with broad avenues, cafés, and shops as one would see in France. I was, of course, attracted to the Medina, the older part of town, and booked a room in a hotel off the large central square, the Jemaa el-Fnaa. I remained for several days exploring the neighborhoods and *souks*—traditional marketplaces—of the old town.

The sprawling public square and nearby souk provided an amazing array of sights, sounds, and smells. It was filled with stalls of every sort, with merchants selling foods, clothing, pottery, artwork, and more. However, I was mostly attracted to the musicians, who were almost always performing on the square. There were many folk traditions in Morocco, due to its many tribes with their own distinct languages and cultures. The Berbers were the most well-known, particularly in Marrakech, but the sounds in the Jemaa el-Fnaa included an amazing variety of indigenous music. Each day I was able to hear music from the Rif mountain people of the north, the Berbers of southern Morocco, and the black African Moroccans of the desert, whose music resembled that of West Africa.

I marveled at the small groups of black African Moroccan musicians whose three-stringed, guitar-like instruments and hand-held percussive instruments created a sound both ancient and tribal but also contained elements and rhythms of African American blues. Every summer Marrakech held a folk festival in which musicians from every part of the country performed their native music. I was fortunate to be in Marrakech that summer for the festival and left it feeling I had experienced something truly remarkable. I was again reminded how the language of music, regardless of tradition, expressed so deeply the feelings of the human soul.

One afternoon, as I was walking through the Jemaa el-Fnaa, I noticed a boy, about ten years old, who wore a beatific expression. It reminded me of the lad I had seen in Herat speaking in tongues the year before. He was standing by three blind men who were sitting in the square chanting "Allah, Allah" as they collected alms. I had seen these blind men chanting every day in the square and was always moved by their devotion. When the boy saw me, he ran over to me and hugged me. I was astonished but knew instinctively that he could somehow see that I too was on the path to God and that I too was interested in God more than anything else. Afterwards, two Moroccan men explained that I was lucky to have had the attention of this boy because he was known to be special and touched by Allah.

After two weeks in Marrakech, I traveled south through the Ourika Valley, which lay east of Marrakech and followed the Ourika River through the red hills and mountains of Berber country toward the desert. I hitchhiked out of Marrakech and made my way to the simple, two-lane road that followed the Ourika River and was flanked by massive, redstone cliffs. The road was not well-traveled and I did a lot of walking. At one point I met some Berber tribes whose language contained percussive sounds I had never heard before. They spoke no French or Arabic and seemed from another world. Farther along the road, I found a house owned by a German man who invited me to stay for the night. It was a modern dwelling for such a remote location but I greatly welcomed a bit of comfort, which included sleeping on a couch, one of the few times I had not slept on the ground since I entered Morocco. The German explained the history of the Ourika Valley to me and told me what I would find as I walked toward the river's source.

The next day a remarkable event occurred. I continued walking south through the valley and was able to get a ride to where the road ended in a mountainous setting where people were evidently living. Since I had started my travels almost four years before, I had been treated so generously by such a wide variety of people that I now expected a warm welcome wherever I traveled. At the foot of the mountain, at the end of the Ourika Valley road, were a group of dark-skinned, impressive-looking Moroccan men. Their faces radiated a clarity and brightness that immediately made me think they were Sufis and that I had come to a hidden Sufi community. My heart beat quickly as I envisioned being welcomed by them and invited into their community. Wasn't this truly why I had come to Morocco?

I approached the men and asked if they had a place I could spend the night. One told me in French that I could not stay there and should go back toward Marrakech. I asked again, thinking he misunderstood me, but again I was refused. In disbelief, I saw no welcome from these men, only a passive indifference. I was forced to grab my bag and walk back toward the road, heading north now, back toward Marrakech. I was in a daze. As I walked I realized that my traveling was over. With a deep clarity, I knew it was time for me to return home and find a role in this world. I needed to help other people. I thought perhaps I should help other young people like myself who were disenchanted with the materialism of American culture and could not adapt to it. I did not know how I was going to do this but I was certain I had to try. I was going back to America. My days on the road were over.

Part II

THE INNER JOURNEY

Chapter 8

ARICA

It took me two weeks to return to Paris where I again stayed with Francois and Nicole and told them my traveling days were over. They listened skeptically. They knew much of my inspiration came from my travels and wondered how I was going to give that up. But I knew my life was about to change. I had to somehow offer myself to this world and contribute something of value.

I returned to America in August 1973 and sought out my friends in Boston. My friend Paul was living in an apartment in Back Bay, near Northeastern University, where he was about to start graduate school. We met briefly and he gave me the keys to his apartment before leaving for New Hampshire to be with his wife before his classes started.

At this point I was at a crossroad and did not know what to do. So I attempted something I had never done before: I prayed. I prayed that God would show me the right path. I prayed that I could be of service to other human beings. I prayed that I could share with others whatever little knowledge I had gained thus far in my life. Mostly I prayed for a teacher to guide me because I realized that, no matter how much I read or heard about spirituality, I did not know much. My prayer came out spontaneously and I felt God received it. I started sitting in on meditation sessions around Boston. I heard swamis teach and Sufis chant and learned about astral traveling. There were so many spiritual paths but none awakened anything special in me. One day at Harvard Square, a young woman offered to read my palm. She looked at my open hand and said, "Oh my, you are ready. I see you in a boat on a stormy sea and you are saying, God direct me!"

I began to sit in on an introductory session given by the spiritual school Arica. I found the Arica instructors appealing. Their teachings reminded me of those of Swami Vivekananda. In a month they were offering a forty-day training—an initiation into the Arica teachings. Since they needed help remodeling their new facility on Boylston Street, they offered the training free if I would work with their crew to complete the remodeling. They were so welcoming that I agreed and started work the next day.

Arica was established in the late 60s in Arica, Chile by the Chilean mystic Oscar Ichazo. He opened the Arica school in the United States in the early 70s. Oscar was a spiritual teacher who had studied under a number of masters from many spiritual traditions, including Gurdjieff. He had mastered several forms of martial arts and was exposed to the teachings of Tibetan Buddhists, Sufis, Indian yogis, Jewish Kabbalists, and Chinese Taoists. He informed us that Arica was an ancient spiritual school that had existed as far back as ancient Egypt. He was not the founder of the school but a living member assisting in its continuance during our time. The practices of Arica included a set of physical exercises and movements borrowed from hatha yoga and Tai Chi, meditation techniques from the Indian yoga and Tibetan Buddhist traditions, and a psychological system based on the Enneagram.

Pervading the atmosphere of the Arica school was an uplifting spiritual energy that made the practices come alive. For the first time, I was able to truly meditate, experiencing inner lights and sounds and a deep inner joy. I became good friends with several others who joined me in the construction work and the forty-day training. It was a diverse group of hippies with big hearts who, like me, were graduating from the fun and freedom of hippie life into a more deliberate and serious focus on spiritual growth.

I took several Arica trainings over a nine-month period in Boston and New York City. After the second training, I moved into a large house on Linnaean Street in Cambridge, off Harvard Square, where, with a dozen other Aricans, I undertook a special three-month training. I also became a teacher for the next forty-day training in Boston.

I felt very much at home in the Arica setting. It offered me an uncomplicated reintroduction into my own culture after four years on the road. It also gave me an instant community of like-minded friends whose interests and pasts were much like my own. I made many good friends in a short time at Arica but there were some problems. Oscar believed the Aricans could monitor their own behavior though the practices he had established and did not institute any type of discipline in the Arica communities formed in the U.S. However, most of the Aricans I knew were emerging from an unrestrained hippie lifestyle that was not easy to give up. An obsession with sex and drugs undermined the spiritual work of several Aricans. It was not pretty to watch. Still, a significant group were more moderate in their approach. For the most part, the year I spent with them was fun and spiritually uplifting.

After the three-month training, I moved to another Arica house in Boston's South End, a grittier part of Boston just starting to gentrify. Suddenly I found that I did not fit in with what was happening in Arica. Oscar introduced new techniques for his spiritual work that I felt little attraction to. I had envisioned studying for many years in Arica until I had mastered the things that Oscar had but it was not to be.

I soon entered into a relationship with a woman named Michaela who was also living in the South End Arica house. Michaela was young and pretty and displayed the carefree, free-loving attitude that permeated hippie culture in those days. I had fantasized about being in a relationship with such a woman but it always seemed just out of reach for me. However, after being with her for a few weeks, I discovered that Michaela's carefree hippie attitude covered up a lot of sadness and uncertainty. There was not a wellspring of joy beneath her tantalizing exterior.

I began to experience a great deal of doubt about my spiritual life. I felt no affinity toward the new Arica practices and feared that my spiritual progress had reached a dead end. At the same time, my relationship with Michaela became less and less satisfying. Needing to earn some money, I took a job as a waiter at a restaurant on Harvard Square. One day, busy taking orders, I heard a man at a nearby table say something about his guru. Drawn by the word "guru," I rushed over to him and asked who his guru was. He wrote down his phone number and told me to call him when I had a chance.

Later that evening I called this man, Jose, who came to meet me at the Arica house. Jose was a short, stocky black man of Hispanic background in his mid-forties who had lived in New York for many years. A highly intelligent man with an effusive personality, he told me how he had met an Indian holy man in New York several years ago and had asked him to be his guru. The guru told Jose that he was too old, with only a few years left to live, and did not think he could be a proper guide for him. But Jose begged, saying he desperately needed a spiritual guide, and the guru finally acquiesced. About a year later, his guru came to Jose in a dream and told him he was leaving his body but would always be there for Jose. A short time later, his guru died. As the years passed, Jose confided in me that, true to his word, his guru appeared and bestowed comfort and grace on him whenever Jose called on him in his meditation or prayers,. He also shared that, at one point, while suffering from severe liver disease, he saw his guru in a dream and was healed of the worst effects of his illness.

I was moved by Jose's story. It reminded me of something Oscar had said in one of his trainings when an Arican asked if Oscar was a guru. Oscar answered emphatically that no, he was not a guru, that a guru was one who, once he began to guide a disciple, never left that disciple and would always be with him and look after him. Oscar explained that he was a brother to all the Aricans in the Arica school but that a guru was quite different.

Jose had psychic abilities. As we continued to see each other, he told me of some of my past lives. He explained that there was a beautiful spiritual energy pervading the Arica house but that this fine energy was being abused by the lack of discipline of the people living there and their attraction to drugs and sex. Most important, Jose confirmed that I would continue to grow spiritually in my life and that other paths would open up to me. I was moved by Jose's words and took it as a sign that God was still looking after me.

Many of the Aricans where I lived were attracted to psychics. One was a woman named Rosemarie, who lived with her husband in the Boston suburbs. Rosemarie belonged to a spiritual path called the White Brotherhood. Along with giving readings, her service was to help people who had died, through accidents or sickness, and found themselves confused in another plane of existence, sometimes not even realizing they had died. She psychically met people on the astral plane and offered guidance so they could move on in their evolution.

I decided to have a reading with Rosemarie. I traveled out to her middle-class apartment in the suburbs, surprised at how un-hippie-like it was. As the reading began, she asked if I admired John F. Kennedy. She explained that John Kennedy was there at the reading and had placed his hands on my shoulders. She said she saw me practicing law and helping many immigrants who had nowhere to turn in America. Her words, surprisingly, resonated deep within me although I had never consciously contemplated going into law before. As she spoke I clearly envisioned myself helping struggling immigrants navigate the obtuse legal pathways in America. I asked her if she saw me continuing my spiritual path with Arica. She was silent for a few moments and then said, "I see a band of Eastern masters surrounding and protecting you." I was not sure what that meant. When I asked Rosemarie if she saw my relationship with Michaela progressing, she suggested that both Michaela and I have dinner with her to determine what would be best for us.

Two weeks later Michaela and I arrived at Rosemarie's apartment for dinner. After hearing about our relationship, Rosemarie urged us to make a strong commitment to each other. She explained that if we did not do so by the next weekend, it would be very difficult for our relationship to continue. I was moved to make this commitment but then remembered I had enrolled in a meditation retreat in the mountains of New York for the following weekend. The retreat was offered by an intriguing spiritual teacher called Guruji. I was greatly attracted to this retreat and for some reason could not consider missing it. I hoped Michaela and I could make our new commitment when I returned.

Chapter 9

GURUJI

It was late October 1974. The countryside in New York's Catskill Mountains, where Guruji was holding his retreat, was filled with apple orchards; the orange, yellow, and red leaves were still clinging to the trees. At each intersection we passed makeshift stands where farmers sold bushels of apples and gallon jars of apple cider. The air was crisp and cool, lightened with the fragrance of apples. In late afternoon I arrived at the retreat site, a small mountain lodge on a beautiful wooded lake, surrounded by cabins where the retreat participants were to sleep. I walked into the lodge to register and noticed at the far end a dark-skinned man dressed in the orange robes of a monk, sporting long, dark hair, a curly beard, and a red ski cap. I looked at him sitting there and could feel his attention turn toward me. Inwardly I heard him say to me, "Ah, so you've come." This was Guruji.

It was a four-day retreat attended by about forty people, most around my age. Guruji was a short, vibrant Indian man of about sixty years who seemed constantly in motion. He sat on a raised chair at the front of the retreat hall where he gave several talks in Hindi, translated by a younger Indian man also wearing the robes of a monk. A powerful spiritual energy emanated from him and pervaded the atmosphere of the retreat. Watching him speak, I was fascinated by his expressiveness as well as his evident good humor. As the retreat progressed, I was overcome by a feeling of deep joy. Several times during meditation sessions, Guruji walked through the retreat hall and placed his hand on the heads of the meditators. When this happened to me, I fell into a deep meditation. Inner lights arose and waves of blissful energy flowed through my body. A sense of wonder grew in me as the retreat went on.

From my Arica practices, I was familiar with experiences of light and spiritual energy in my meditation. Nonetheless, I was captivated by the power of this new manifestation of spiritual energy and the ease with which it seemed to emanate from Guruji and enter me. Guruji also led several rousing chants in the Sanskrit language that seemed to open my heart and release the tensions I held in my mind and body.

During the retreat I became aware of a group doing all the work, busily taking registrations, cooking meals, and cleaning the meditation and dining halls. They did not seem as carefree as the people attending the retreat and I wondered what motivated them to work so hard without experiencing the delights of the event.

After dinner the first day, walking back to my lodging, I saw Guruji sitting in a chair outside of his cabin, surrounded by these workers. They were sitting on the ground around him, silently watching him. I too sat in the circle, waiting for him to speak. After some time I grew restless. Suddenly Guruji looked directly at me and my mind became completely still. Feelings of joy arose with this mental stillness, along with waves of unconditional love coming from Guruji. I had not experienced this type of love before, though I recognized it for what it was. I learned afterwards that I had just experienced *darshan*, the opportunity to sit in the presence of a spiritual master and experience his elevated state. After receiving this blessing from Guruji, I no longer wondered why those doing the work at the retreat were so willing to offer their service to him.

Guruji's teachings at the retreat were simple: meditate on and honor your own inner being; recognize that your own inner being is God. I had been exposed to these teachings during my travels in India from my readings of Swami Vivekananda. Lanza del Vasto had also adopted these teachings from his time with Gandhi. They were at the core of the yoga tradition in India. Yet I found Guruji's formulation unique and distinct in a way I could not yet describe. After leaving the retreat, I pondered his teachings but mostly left remarkably impressed by his presence, the powerful spiritual energy that emanated from him, and the extraordinary experiences I had in meditation.

Returning to Boston I found that Michaela had slept with another man in my absence. It didn't surprise me since the Arican culture was one of free love and Michaela embodied this more than others. But I felt hurt and betrayed. Nevertheless, I soon found myself relieved to be free of this entanglement. Being with Guruji had reawakened my desire to grow spiritually and I now wanted to focus my attention in this direction.

I moved into my own smaller room at the Arica house and began to pursue my new spiritual practices. I set up an altar similar to ones I had seen at the retreat, with a picture of Guruji, a candle, and incense, and began to devote time each day to meditation, reading Guruji's books, and listening to recordings of his chants. Performing these practices, the same energy I had experienced at the retreat flowed through me and began to pervade my room. After a few days, drawn by the energy, several Aricans began coming to my room to meditate and chant with me.

In late December 1974, Guruji came to Boston to give a public program and two-day retreat. The retreat took place at a small college in Cambridge and held about fifty people. It was similar to the one I had attended in New York, with long mediation sessions, talks on spirituality by Guruji, and several rousing chants. During one of the meditation sessions, as I sat with my eyes closed, Guruji came and placed his hand on the top of my head for several seconds. I felt his energy course through my body from head to toe, an unconditional love that flowed through every part of my being. I felt totally accepted by Guruji and fully loved for what I was. It seemed he was saying to me, "You are mine now."

Guruji was staying at the Arica house in Cambridge, where I had lived the year before. In the evenings after the retreat, I went there hoping to have his darshan. Here I became familiar with his playful side. Many influential spiritual teachers in the Boston area came to meet Guruji in the evenings for short individual sessions, which I was able to observe. One such teacher was an erudite Japanese man who had established a school for macrobiotic cooking in Boston. After his interview Guruji offered him a bar of chocolate and a large bag of basmati rice, considered the finest in India. I was acutely aware that people following the macrobiotic diet did not eat sugar or white rice. However, in India, when a spiritual master gives the gift of food it is considered a blessing. I saw the puzzled expression on the Japanese man's face as he attempted to reconcile Guruji's gift of food with his strict formulation of what was good to eat and what was not. I delighted in seeing how Guruji playfully worked on the mental limitations people assume in the name of spirituality.

Learning that Guruji would be holding a retreat in Hawaii in March 1975, I flew to Honolulu in February to join him there. He arrived in Honolulu at the beginning of March and stayed at a small house on the beach. It was an exquisite setting, overlooking the ocean and surrounded by palm trees and the beautiful flowering plants of Hawaii. In the living room, Guruji gave daily programs from early morning to late at night. About forty people gathered at the house at four each morning for meditation and remained there most of the day, taking meals and sitting in on Guruji's talks, question-and-answer sessions, chants, and darshan. The atmosphere was personal and intimate. Guruji paid a good deal of attention to each one of us during the month.

The first people I met at Guruji's house were Durga and Kalyani, the Australian women who had been at Swami Premvarni's ashram in Rishikesh and had helped guide me through the intricacies of life there. We recognized each other immediately. They were not surprised to see me there. Durga said that true seekers eventually find a true spiritual teacher to guide them. A third person from Swami Premvarni's ashram was also there: a young man who played the Indian drum for Guruji's chanting sessions. I was struck by the apparent "coincidence" of meeting these women at two important stages of my spiritual search.

In my early-morning meditation sessions, an inner spiritual work of purification began that would last several years. Although I outwardly had lived a carefree hippie lifestyle during my college and traveling days, I was filled with vague, painful feelings from my past I was barely aware of. During the morning meditations, this emotional pain concealed within me arose like a gale sweeping through my body and mind, making me cry out with pain. At the same time, I felt remarkably detached from the pain, as if I were watching from a distance. By the end of each session, the feelings of emotional pain subsided and I came out of meditation feeling cleansed, refreshed, and radiating with joy. This repeated itself each day I was with Guruji that month in Hawaii. One afternoon I asked Guruji what was happening to me in my meditation. He explained that the pain of feeling separate from God, of feeling alone and vulnerable, had created an inner anguish that left deep impressions of despair in me that had become habitual. I had become identified with these feelings and thought they *were* me. Now God's energy was moving through me, bringing my emotional blocks to the surface to be seen and dispelled. The inner divine light of my true nature was beginning to arise.

One thing that initially confused me, sitting with Guruji, was the difference between the practices I had learned in Arica, which

I still found beneficial, and the new ones Guruji taught. I asked him if I should continue my Arica practices or just focus on the new practices I was learning from him. He gave a deep chuckle and responded, "Don't worry! I am the Arica House!" I spent a lot of time trying to understand his words and finally concluded he meant that, as my guru, he encompassed the teachings and practices of all paths that led to divine realization, no matter the outer form.

The third week of the retreat was in Maui at a remote campsite in the mountains, on the northeastern tip of the island, overlooking the ocean. The retreat took place in a lodge surrounded by several cottages where the participants slept. One evening, after the retreat program, I took a walk down one of the mountain paths as the sun was setting, the ocean slowly disappearing from view as evening grew darker. A fine rain was falling, creating a mist that blanketed the hills. Reaching the end of the pathway, I turned back and noticed that Guruji was walking directly toward me. I sought something interesting to say to him and imagined he was doing the same. However, as he approached, I could see from his eyes that, far from thinking about me, he was immersed in his divine inner state and was repeating his mantra while he worked his *japa mala*. As he was almost upon me, I said, "Hi Guruji," and he suddenly stopped and looked at me with eyes full of divine intoxication and said simply, "Hullo!" From that one word, a powerful spiritual energy spread through me and I experienced Guruji's state of divine love pulsating through my body. Looking at Guruji, I remembered Sri Ramakrishna, the great Indian saint I had read about in India, whose sole desire was to be immersed in the love of God. I had wondered if the world still had teachers such as Ramakrishna and had prayed to be able to meet such a one. Now I realized that my prayer had been answered.

Before leaving Hawaii I was able to meet with Guruji to tell him about my reading with Rosemarie in which she saw me practicing law. I asked Guruji if I should consider going to law school. He looked at me in a piercing way and asked how long it would take.

When I told him four years, he made a dismissive gesture that I interpreted as, "No, it would take too long." I understood this to mean that it was important for me to be with Guruji these next years; I would not get another chance. Then, surprisingly, Guruji said, "But law would be good for you!"

At the end of my stay in Hawaii, I asked Guruji if I could serve him though I had no idea what that meant. He smiled and told me I should go to the new ashram he was opening in California and meet him there. Excited with the anticipation of living in an ashram, I flew to California to await Guruji's arrival.

Chapter 10

ASHRAM

O ur days began with meditation at 4:30 a.m. in the large meditation hall. I quickly became acquainted with the special qualities the early morning has for meditators. A deep silence pervaded the hall, pregnant with the divine spiritual energy I now associated with Guruji. The hall was dark except for candles placed on the altars on either side of Guruji's chair. Large pictures of enlightened masters from the Indian tradition graced the walls around the hall. In front of Guruji's chair, a woman chanted a beautiful and haunting prayer in Sanskrit, accompanying herself on harmonium. She was joined by another woman playing tamboura, adding the meditative drone of Indian music. After a few minutes, the chant ended and we were left in a thick silence, drawn into the deep state of meditation that seemed to arise spontaneously wherever Guruji was present. After an hour of deep meditation, a gong sounded and we slowly arose, renewed and enlivened by the divine energy coursing through our beings. It was still dark as we made our way to morning tea and sat in silence awaiting the early morning chant.

I was now living in an ashram under the guidance of Guruji in an urban setting on the fringe of a ghetto area in northern California. My days revolved around a continuous schedule of meditation, chanting, and *ashram seva*—selfless service that teaches one how to offer work in this world with love. It all left little time for anything else. Yet within this restrictive schedule, a new inner world was opening up for me, a world of inner lights, sounds, and visions. I was also introduced to the esoteric philosophies of ancient India. At the center of everything was Guruji: his daily darshan, his teachings, and the ecstatic, divine energy emanating from him.

The first sevas I was given were physical and rudimentary. They revolved around the simple tasks of life that, for many years, I had considered unimportant. I cleaned dishes, mopped hallways, vacuumed bedrooms and offices, scoured toilets, and swept sidewalks. I served food, chopped vegetables, drove people here and there, and stood duty as a security guard. I answered the telephone, watered the garden, and blew a conch at 4:00 a.m. to awaken ashramites for morning meditation. At first I found the work tedious and could not wait for it to end so I could get back to my spiritual practices. I wondered when I would be given a seva where I could use my intellect.

From the beginning Guruji had me earn my keep at the ashram. Although there were many in the ashram doing seva who were given free room and board, Guruji asked me to find outside, part-time work to pay for my room and board. For several months I worked in a hospital kitchen, later at a tomato cannery. I was certain I was doing penance for the years of my hippie lifestyle, when I had worked as little as possible. Later I saw that Guruji's instructions had a deeper purpose that bore unexpected fruit. Still, the room and board was inexpensive and it proved easy enough for me to earn my keep and still have an active life in the ashram.

In August 1975 Guruji gave a month-long retreat at a college

campus in the mountains of northern California. The campus was
an ideal retreat spot, with a gymnasium converted into a large
meditation hall, a large kitchen and cafeteria to feed hundreds, and
dorm rooms that were modern and luxurious compared to the simple
rooms at the California ashram. The campus was set in the Sierras,
surrounded by redwoods and groves of eucalyptus trees. People from
all over the world came to be with Guruji for the month.

One morning, while chanting with hundreds of people, I recalled
a good friend from college who had committed suicide while I was
living in Paris. I felt tremendous remorse for his death and terrible
guilt that I had not been there for him. Pain rose up strongly in me
and, before long, torrents of tears were running down my face. Then
the pain of my friend's suicide turned into something deeper: the
existential pain of my life feeling separate from God; deep feelings of
unworthiness; feelings of being alone and alienated from the world.
As these painful emotions washed through me, I left the meditation
hall so as not to disturb the others. Miserably I walked across the
hilly, forested campus and gradually came to the apartment where
Guruji was staying. I did not intentionally seek out Guruji but was
somehow drawn to him irresistibly, as if pulled by a string. At the
foot of the steps leading up to his apartment, I felt the string keep
pulling me up the steps to the deck leading to his apartment. At
the top I saw Guruji on the walkway about to turn the corner and
I cried out to him.

Guruji turned and saw me. A flash of recognition crossed his face
and in an instant he was there before me. Lying on the walkway, I
grasped his feet and held on, barely knowing why I was there except
for the pain in my heart. Slowly my mind became quiet as I lay there
holding Guruji's feet. After several minutes I heard him say to me
inwardly, "Follow the path I have to show you and you will attain
what you wish to attain." With those words, I released Guruji's feet
and, looking out, saw that hundreds of people had gathered around
watching the spectacle of me in tears holding Guruji's feet. Then

Guruji had two men help me to my feet and take me to my room. I was charged with so much spiritual energy that I could barely walk.

Soon I realized that something had fundamentally changed within me from this experience. Most obvious was that, for the first time, a sincere desire to be of service took hold of me. Whatever hesitations I once had about doing ashram seva were now replaced by a desire to do whatever I could to help Guruji in his work. More mysteriously, I felt closer to Guruji, as if a layer of separation between us had been dissolved. With some reflection I came to understand that, without a formal ceremony, Guruji had given me an initiation and through this I had become his disciple.

As my time with Guruji progressed, I began to get insights into the nature of the guru-disciple relationship, which existed on many levels. There was the obvious outer relationship where Guruji taught me through words, instructions, and physical interactions. But there was also a much deeper inner relationship in which I gradually became aware that the essence of the guru and that of my own self were one and the same. This inner relationship became more and more important as I proceeded on my spiritual path.

I spent a lot of time in Guruji's presence that year, sometimes listening to him give teachings and at other times just sitting with him in relative silence. During the silent times, as I sat and watched Guruji, the powerful vibration of his spiritual energy resonated within me, strengthening a conscious awareness of my own divine essence. Day after day I sat with him as this awareness became stronger and stronger. In this way I came to understand one of the fundamental teachings of the ancient Indian scriptures: *Aham Brahmasmi*—I am Brahman, I am the Absolute. With a clear experience of the Absolute now within me, I was more easily able to distinguish those aspects of myself not of that essence and realize that they were not in fact me. Profound spiritual understandings begin to arise and I marveled at how fortunate I was to be with such a spiritual master.

I continued to do seva at the California ashram after the retreat, now with a feeling of deep joy. The ashramites I was with were a unique and diverse group and many close friendships began in those days. Those who assumed leadership roles were, for the most part, older, with various levels of professional experience. They were professors, psychologists, actors, lawyers, and so on. But there were also construction workers, electricians, plumbers, and cooks. One of my first roommates was a former professional football player. Men and women of all colors, races, and religions came from Europe, Latin America, and India to live in the ashram. It seemed to me an ideal community. I remembered how I had often yearned to be part of a community of like-minded souls, bonded in love with a common purpose to serve and help others. Now I was part of such a community.

In February 1976, after I'd spent nine months in California, Guruji sent me with a group of other sevites to open a new ashram in the mountains of New York. For three months I immersed myself in the joyful work of converting an old hotel into an ashram. When Guruji arrived in May, he told us he would be traveling back to India at the end of the summer. If we wished to join him, we needed funds for our airfare and room and board. Several of us got jobs as waiters and waitresses in the surrounding Catskill mountain hotels so we could travel to India with Guruji in October.

Chapter 11

ASHRAM IN INDIA

I n October 1976 I flew to India with over one hundred devotees
to join Guruji at his home ashram in India. We flew into the
antiquated Mumbai Airport at the end of the Indian monsoon
season and were met with dark puddles of standing water in the
corridors and lavatories. Mumbai was humid and hot, exuding both
the rich scents of the blossoming flowers and the inevitable smells
of manure and feces that always seemed present in India. Sanitation
had not changed since my last visit. We arrived in darkness at 2:00
a.m. Indian time but by the time we were through customs and had
boarded the buses to the ashram the sun was bright in the sky and
the morning traffic had begun. It was a three-hour ride from the
airport to Navsari. The narrow two-lane highway was crammed with
trucks and buses spewing black clouds of exhaust. For several miles
the road also served as the main thoroughfare through the suburbs
that spread north of Mumbai. It was jammed with pedestrians going

about their daily affairs. After two hours of bumpy, stop-and-go traffic, we turned inland onto a smaller country road with little traffic that cut through several s with green, flooded rice paddies. Indian men and women worked in the paddies up to their knees in water. At last, to our left, the ashram rose above the fields and we finally turned onto the road to the ashram and town of Navsari.

The ashram's simple beauty and cleanliness made it stand out from anything I had previously seen in India. We entered a gateway that led to a marble-tiled courtyard in which stood several flowering trees. The fragrance of champa blossoms surrounded us as we were met by several Westerners who had been living in Navsari during the years Guruji had been in America. They looked thin and weathered, though they were also radiant with the wonderful light always present in Guruji's ashrams.

A new dormitory of red brick and cement had been constructed during Guruji's absence to house the expected surge of Westerners. My room contained five Indian-style beds, lockers for clothes, and a little balcony overlooking the rice paddies of the neighboring village. The bathrooms and showers were communal and located down the hall. My roommates were a diverse bunch from the U.S. and Europe.

The ashram was exquisite. The buildings surrounding the courtyard included a large temple, a meditation veranda, and a group of offices above which were dormitories for men and women. Around one side of the courtyard was a large dining hall and kitchen and on the other side was a communal bathhouse of stalls with waist-high taps and buckets with which to bathe. Beyond were fields of rice paddies separating the main part of the ashram from the upper gardens where there was a small Shiva temple, a large pavilion for fire ceremonies, a rose garden, and other assorted buildings. The beautiful winding pathways that led through the upper gardens were adorned with statues of yogis and mythical figures from the Indian spiritual tradition.

After two days of getting acclimated, I was selected to work in the kitchen and dining hall. A tall, young American from Brooklyn named Mel was chosen as our seva leader and I became his assistant. The ashram kitchen had never had a foreigner work in it before and our presence created a controversy. Some of the older Indian devotees were opposed to anyone but Brahmins cooking the ashram's food. Guruji then brought in a respected Indian yogi from Rishikesh to oversee the kitchen work and help acclimate the Indian devotees to the new Western help.

I was determined to make the most of my stay at the ashram and made up my mind to strictly follow the ashram schedule. The days were long and filled with a variety of practices. Morning meditation started at 4:00 a.m. so I was up by 3:15 a.m. each day. I spent several hours a day doing my work in the kitchen and dining hall, helping wash and chop the food for the cooks, rolling chapatis, serving meals to the ashram residents and guests, and keeping the kitchen and dining hall spotlessly clean.

I felt totally at home in the ashram kitchen. The kitchen and dining hall were constructed simply, with gray stone floors and whitewashed walls. The food was cooked on massive coal-burning stoves over which stood huge metal pots that held our daily fare of dal, spiced vegetables, and rice. The chapatis were also cooked on a grill over the fires. The meals were served on a traditional round metal *thali*, or platter. Everyone sat on the dining hall floor in parallel rows eating the food with their hands, in silence. There were no kitchen utensils in those days. I was struck by how content and fulfilled I felt just preparing and serving the food and sweeping and mopping the floors. I also felt a special affinity to the Indian kitchen staff. Although we did not speak the same language, as we worked together over several months we developed a close bond. I always felt welcome and at ease with them.

When I had free time, I walked the mile down the road to the town of Navsari where Guruji's guru Bapuji was buried and where Bapuji's old ashram was maintained. The town was located in the Vapi valley, a poor rural section of the state of Maharashtra that had not yet seen the urban changes sweeping Mumbai, only forty miles away. The valley was inhabited mostly by Adivasis, poor and uneducated Indian tribal people descended from the aboriginal inhabitants of India. Flowing through the valley was a meandering river, which provided most of the water for the valley. It flowed with a strong current in the monsoon season, often flooding, and slowed to a trickle during the hot, dry season. In the midst of the river at several spots were sulfurous hot springs with reputed healing properties. Some of the villages had rest houses where visitors could stay to bathe in the hot springs. The valley was pervaded with rice paddies, small plots for growing fruits and vegetables, and wandering cows, goats, and water buffalo. Most of the villagers lived in mud dwellings with thatched roofs; the village women carried large pots of water on their heads from the river to their homes while men drove their bullock carts, slowly ambling along the narrow, rutted roads.

Walking into Navsari was like walking into another world in a century long past. Gone was the cleanliness, quietude, and beauty of Guruji's ashram, replaced by the raucous street noise of the town, the pungent smells of Indian cooking and animal manure along the unpaved streets, and the ubiquitous wandering of emaciated cows. I normally went first to Bapuji's samadhi shrine, where he was buried, to offer a garland of flowers to his image and sit in meditation. It was a spiritually charged place carrying the divine vibration of Guruji's guru.

I would then visit Bapuji's ashram where he had lived the last years of his life. Unlike the samadhi shrine, his ashram was visited by few pilgrims, leaving it in a state of simplicity and quietude. The energy of Bapuji was also powerful here. The ashram was built simply with stone floors and whitewashed walls. It contained a platform where Bapuji had slept, a chair in which he had sat, and a hall in which he had given darshan. While Bapuji was alive, millions of Indians came from all over India to have his darshan in this tiny ashram.

In the opposite direction from Guruji's ashram, following the

winding course of the river, was the town of Sonali, which held
an ancient temple dedicated to the *Devi*, or divine mother. Guruji
lived in a room in this temple for some years during the time of
his *sadhana*—his spiritual practices. Like Navsari, Sonali was a
poor and dirty town, yet it held within itself a spiritual treasure.
The temple sat on a hill overlooking the whole Vapi valley. It had
a courtyard leading into the inner sanctum where there were three
small Devi statues covered in flowers and dotted with kumkum
and ash. The spiritual energy emanating from these statues was
surprisingly powerful, making me wonder at the spiritual power
hidden in India's simplest settings.

As the Indian winter approached, our morning meditation
and chanting sessions took on a different quality. The cooler, drier
weather offered a welcome respite from the long months of intense
heat and humidity. Meditation was held in a u-shaped, open-air hall
that surrounded Guruji's original room in the ashram. For these
early-morning meditation and chanting sessions, we all bundled up
in our coats and shawls, blissfully welcoming the cool winter Indian
air. After meditation and the morning Arati chant, we lined up in
the dining hall for hot cups of chai and sat on the floor in silence,
delighting in the after-effects of our morning practices. Then we
proceeded to the courtyard to chant a scriptural text with Guruji
during which the sun gradually rose over the surrounding hills and
began to fill the courtyard with its splendid light and warmth. These
sessions were filled with Guruji's presence and caused us to radiate
with the vibrations of divine light coursing through our bodies and
minds.

As the months passed, I became more dedicated to my spiritual
practices and seva. Occasionally, on holidays, thousands of Indians
came to celebrate. During the celebrations Guruji held eight-day
chants in a temple in the upper gardens. Men and women alternated
in twelve-hour shifts as the ashram was suffused with the divine
sound of melodious chanting. Often meals served during these
celebrations ran for several hours as we attempted to feed thousands

of Indian visitors. At the end of the eight-day session, Guruji held
a finale in which everyone, men and women, participated in the
closing chants. The energy was powerful and ecstatic.

At one point, as winter receded and the weather became warmer,
I started feeling weak from the strict routine I had been following
for months, a condition that was exacerbated by occasional bouts
of dysentery. I had been getting up at 3:00 a.m. every morning and
doing all of the practices and seva I could, not considering the needs
of my body for balance and rest. As a result my time at the ashram
began to take on a feeling of intense austerity.

One afternoon, feeling I needed a break, I walked into Navsari
to visit Bapuji's ashram. On entering I saw with surprise that a large
crowd had gathered and was surrounding a young yogi with long
dark hair and a striking face. I asked who this sadhu was and was
told he had been a devotee of Bapuji since he was a child and was
now considered a holy man with his own ashram a few villages away.
Suddenly a group of the devotees grabbed me by the arm and rushed
me to this sadhu for darshan. I respectfully bowed at his feet and,
rising, looked into his eyes. Unexpectedly I was pierced with a divine
white light that left me dazed, barely able to stand up. I was helped
to a seat where I sat disoriented and surprised for several minutes.

I walked back to the ashram thinking about how I was doing all
of these sevas and spiritual practices, working myself to the point of
exhaustion, and this yogi looked at me for just a second and filled me
with divine light! Why was I doing all of this work and exhausting
myself? As I entered the ashram, I found Guruji standing at the far
side of the courtyard. He took a look at me and seemed to chuckle.
Seeing him there, understanding suddenly arose in me. I knew
he could always give me that divine state in an instant. In fact he
had many times. But my problem was the mental tendencies that
continued to bring me back to my limited consciousness. I was again
reminded of my deeper commitment to my practices and vowed to
conscientiously follow the path Guruji had laid out for me.

As March turned into April and the weather became hot again, my health problems increased. The heat, with daily temperatures well over one hundred degrees, wore down my body, leaving me feeling depleted and exhausted. Then, in short order, I came down with intestinal parasites followed by shingles, a painful virus that attached itself to the nerves of my stomach. It was so painful that for weeks I could not wear a shirt.

A few weeks before his birthday celebrations in May 1977, Guruji announced that he would be holding a ceremony to convey monkhood, or *sanyasa*, to several of his Western disciples. Two of my close friends were chosen to receive the initiation, causing me to deeply ponder if I too wanted to become a monk. I was now intensely drawn to a spiritual life and the desire to serve others but did not know, in practical terms, what a lifelong commitment to monkhood meant.

As the birthday celebrations arrived, thousands of visitors began to flood the ashram. In honor of the occasion, Guruji held a five-day fire ceremony, or *yajna*, led by a distinguished group of elder Brahman priests. I had never witnessed a yajna before and was surprised by its power and depth. It is an ancient Vedic ritual in which, from sunrise to sunset, the priests offer sacred objects into the burning fire, representing the divine source of all, while chanting Vedic mantras continuously in perfect unison. The smell of burning ghee and sacred woods and herbs, combined with the powerful mantras of the Brahman priests, filled the ashram, creating a divine and still atmosphere that permeated the grounds.

As the Brahmans offered the precious materials into the fire, those of us observing were guided to mentally offer to the fire every part of our being—our good and bad qualities, our desires and goals, talents and strengths, as well as our weaknesses. As the Brahmans chanted, we slowly walked around the fire pit listening attentively to the mantras, feeling the heat rise from the fire, imbibing the smells of the burning substances, and feeling it on our skins. Continuing to walk, we offered our very beings to the sacred source of all. In that offering I became absorbed into a divine state of oneness, intoxicated with the divine energy of the yajna and feeling cleansed, as if the fire was burning to ashes the latent impurities of my mind and body that had been with me for lifetimes. As the yajna progressed, I began to feel emptied of everything but the divine light within.

Along with the yajna, Guruji also led a sanyasa initiation ceremony in a separate part of the ashram where the initiates were also asked to offer their entire beings to God and to renounce every part of themselves external to their divine inner nature. After renouncing all they were led to the river where they entered without clothes, signifying that they had left all worldly attachments behind. They then began walking in the direction of the Himalayas, symbolizing a life of renunciation. However, the presiding monk then called to them to return so they could offer their lives in service to humanity. Although I did not take part in the sanyas ceremony, its power and vibration pervaded the ashram and flowed through me in a personal way, giving me a strong inner urge to dedicate my life in service to God and all beings. In feeling this I recognized it as something deeply familiar. I wondered in how many past lives I had taken these vows.

The ceremonies had a profound effect on me. They also marked the end of my stay in Navsari. My funds were nearly depleted and my health compromised. Guruji indicated that I should return to the ashram in California and wait for him there. He would be returning for his next tour to America in a year. I left Navsari reluctantly. I had never experienced such a holy place before. I would miss its high, refined vibration, its simplicity and beauty and my wonderful experiences. I would also miss the divine presence of my guru who was for me an embodiment of divine love, wisdom, and compassion. For the first time in two years, I would now be spending time away from him.

Chapter 12

MY DARK NIGHT

Returning to America was difficult. My weight dropped to a mere one hundred six pounds and my digestion was still not functioning properly. But, most noticeably, I had a difficult time adjusting to the sudden absence of the high vibration of Navsari, the divine white light that permeated my being for the past eight months. Because of my poor health, I was not asked to do much in the California ashram, which added a feeling of uselessness to my deepening despondency.

Then I read a book—a spiritual classic—called *Dark Night of the Soul* by St. John of the Cross. In it he describes a stage of spiritual life where everything external seems to be taken away from a seeker, leaving an intense feeling of vulnerability. At the same time, the inner light grows increasingly so that the seeker's attention is drawn more to his own divinity than to external matters. This description had an immediate effect on me. I realized that I was still judging my self-worth by the roles I was playing in the ashram, whether or not I felt they were important. Now, back in America, there were basically no roles for me due to my health and as a result I felt rather worthless. However, looking inward, I was intensely aware of the growing light burning within me. Focusing on that light, I knew God was there with me, transforming me from within. With this new understanding, my despondency left. A deeper appreciation of my spiritual process began to emerge.

Guruji returned to America a year later for a three-year tour. By this time I was healthy again and able to contribute by offering seva. As always I worked outside the ashram to earn my keep. Sometimes this made me feel like an outsider when I compared myself to others who spent all their time in service. Still, when I focused inside, the light was there and growing. I tried to remember that this was what was important.

After a year in America Guruji announced that he would be initiating another group of sanyasis during his stay in America. My name was on the list of potential candidates. Soon several meetings were arranged for the candidates and we were given instructions on how to prepare.

One of the tasks given me by Guruji was to memorize two Sanskrit scriptural texts from the tradition of Kashmir Shaivism: the *Shiva Sutras* by Vasugupta Charya and the *Pratyabhijna Hrdayam* by Ksemeraj. I was instructed to focus on memorization rather than studying the meaning of the texts. At first it seemed an impossible task. The *Siva Sutras* consisted of seventy-seven verses and the *Pratyabhijna Hrdayam* another twenty. I made note cards for each sutra, which I carried with me wherever I went, and slowly began to memorize them.

After some time I realized that Guruji was initiating me into the deeper meanings of the sutras. The Sanskrit words and syllables began to act as seeds within my psyche, slowly sprouting to reveal profound meanings. A deep joy accompanied the unfolding of these sutras within my mind as the syllables themselves began to teach me, each

Sanskrit root having its own unique force and meaning. Gradually the texts became absorbed into my consciousness, providing an inner structure that shaped my perception of the world. Within me now was an inner conviction that I was an embodiment of divine consciousness creating my own world, similar to how the Creator manifests his creation on the universal scale. I continued to live as an aspiring monk during Guruji's tour of America, waking up early each morning for meditation, chanting the scriptural texts at their appointed times, studying the philosophic texts of our tradition, and doing a variety of sevas to keep the tour running. As per Guruji's instructions, I also continued to earn my keep with part-time work outside the ashram.

In September 1980, while in Los Angeles, Guruji announced that the sanyasa initiations would be held. To my surprise I found that I was no longer on the list of candidates, even though I'd spent the last two years preparing for the initiation. The temporary ashram in Los Angeles consisted of connecting motels overlooking the Pacific Ocean and the Santa Monica beach. A huge tent that held over two thousand people had been constructed on a parking lot for public programs and workshops. It was a beautiful site. The ocean breeze swept through the ashram, carrying its delicate, salty texture throughout the grounds. One evening, after a public program, as Guruji was making his way back to his apartment, I decided to personally ask if I could take sanyasa in the upcoming ceremony. It was a balmy, quiet evening, already dark, when I found Guruji walking to his rooms. As he started to pass me, I approached and asked, "Guruji, can I take sanyasa?"

Guruji turned, grabbed my arm, and smiled deeply. "How long have you been with me?" he asked, still holding my arm.

I responded, "Five years, Guruji."

"Ah, five years," he said. "Very good! Yes, you can take sanyasa!"

Overjoyed, I asked if I could take vows in the upcoming ceremony. But before he could answer, his attention was drawn to another man nearby. Guruji abruptly walked over to him, spoke a few words with him, and then started walking back toward his apartment, paying no attention to me. As he entered his apartment, I called in desperation, "Guruji, sanyasa?"

He stopped, turned toward me with an inscrutable smile, and said, "Next time, in India." He then entered his rooms.

I was in shock. Being left out of the initiation, I hit rock bottom. At the deepest level, I had faith that Guruji knew what was best for me and I gamely tried to fight through feelings of rejection. But waves of unworthiness overcame me. It was a battle to stay positive.

Then, in February, at celebrations for an Indian holiday, Guruji held a long chant with over two thousand people attending under the massive tent. At the end of the chant, he left the hall and as he walked past me I heard him say to me inwardly, "Get ready!" The next day I was told I was to be manager of a new ashram in Washington, DC. Within days I was placed in an intense training program to learn the fundamentals of ashram management. Soon I was on my way to D.C.

Chapter 13

MY EXPANSION

I arrived in Washington, D.C. in July 1980, in the middle of a hot, humid summer. I was met at the airport by Shivaji, a friend who had recently become a monk and now led the new D.C. ashram. The stately ashram building was located on a busy street filled with embassies of smaller countries like Liberia and Cambodia. The building itself had served as the Nicaraguan Embassy for many years. A group of wealthy devotees in D.C. had purchased the ashram so the community could have a large center in which to meditate, chant, and do seva. It was a beautiful older building with a large mediation hall, rooms that could accommodate twenty residents, a large kitchen, and an office.

For the first time since my seva in Navsari, I experienced a significant expansion of my outer role in the ashram. It was intoxicating to feel that my talents were being used again. I eagerly assisted in creating the new ashram schedule, developing courses and programs for the community, and organizing the ashram sevas. Guruji had often repeated a saying from the Vedas: "Only he who obeys can command." I looked back over the past years in which I had committed myself to serving in the ashram regardless of my outer role. I realized that a deep inner work had taken place during this period, too subtle for me to understand intellectually but which allowed me to take this next step in my spiritual growth.

I quickly bonded with Shivaji in our effort to create an inspiring spiritual center in D.C. He was a kind, intelligent monk in his early thirties who was becoming recognized as a distinguished spiritual teacher in his own right. Like me, he had traveled to Paris after his college years and later journeyed throughout the East, slowly becoming an ardent spiritual seeker. He eventually studied Zen Buddhism at a monastery in Kyoto, Japan. While there he read one of Guruji's books and was deeply moved. Frustrated by years of dry practices, he moved to California in 1975 to live and study under Guruji. Because of our similar backgrounds, we worked well together. Years later I saw in meditation that he had been my spiritual teacher in a past life in Japan. I had been there at his death as one of his disciples.

What I liked about Shivaji was that, along with being a mentor, he was a friend. As I observed how he related to the members of the D.C. community, I saw that he acted as a friend to almost everyone. This resonated in me because I too wanted to be a friend to all beings. This was why I wanted to become a monk. There was no doubt in my mind that I was on this earth to realize this desire. Within months of opening in D.C., the ashram had become a vibrant spiritual center for a large community of seekers. The ashram quickly filled with residents and soon we rented a second house down the block for more residents to live. There was a lot of joy in our community due to the ashram's quick growth.

In my new role, I was eager to begin teaching courses in meditation and yoga philosophy. I had studied a great deal during my years with Guruji and had a deep desire to share what I had learned. However, I found teaching more difficult than I imagined. On tour with Guruji, I had been critical of some of Guruji's teachers, seeing their faults and believing I could do better. Now I saw that I had underestimated what it took to teach night after night regardless of my state of mind. Teaching involved more than intellectual understanding or inspired thoughts. It required a balanced mind able to maintain a steadiness regardless of outer circumstances. I witnessed that steadiness in Shivaji and realized that I had a lot of work to do to attain that balance. My time learning to teach became like a mirror reflecting insecurities still below the surface of my conscious mind.

Nevertheless, my stay in D.C. was a time of creativity and expansion. It offered me the chance to express myself in ways that would have been impossible in the larger ashram structure with Guruji. But mostly I cherished the deep connections I made in the D.C. community. The *sangha*, or spiritual community, continued to be a vital part of my spiritual path. I found it a remarkable blessing to live with a group of people in such an atmosphere of love and acceptance. In D.C. I met many who would become lifelong friends and who would share the spiritual path with me for years to come.

I also began to prepare myself mentally for the upcoming sanyasa ceremony to be held in Navsari during Guruji's birthday celebrations. I was one of a few who would be newly initiated. My anticipation grew daily as I pictured myself in the robes of a monk, dedicated to a life of teaching and serving others.

One morning in March 1982, Shivaji called me into his room to speak with him. He looked somber. He had just received a message from Guruji in India saying that I should not take sanyasa in May but wait for the next ceremony. Shivaji was acutely aware how much I desired to become a monk and did his best to soften the message. It was as if the floor fell out from beneath me; I was devastated though I bravely strove not to show it. My understanding of myself during the past years was totally entwined with my desire to be a monk. I could not comprehend what was happening. Disappointment and unworthiness surged through me as I tried to stay mentally afloat.

In late April Shivaji traveled to Navsari for the ceremony and returned the following month. For several months I was despondent, feeling excluded and unworthy. I did not question Guruji's decision but could not help thinking that there was some lack in me that had caused it. Then, to complicate matters, I began to have an attraction toward one of the ashram women. A group of us were meeting daily to oversee management of the ashram and, being in proximity with this woman day after day, I slowly developed a crush on her. On the one hand I enjoyed the feelings awakening in me. But as an aspiring monk I was chagrined and embarrassed to be feeling them. I did not share my feelings with Shivaji, thinking he would only conclude that Guruji had been right in not making me a monk. I kept it tightly inside.

Several months passed. In October of 1982, we were holding a weekend retreat for center leaders from nearby communities in Maryland and Virginia. At the close of the retreat I went to my room to rest before dinner when Shivaji suddenly rushed in.

"Come quickly," he said. "We've got to meet. Guruji took *mahasamadhi!*" Guruji had left is physical body.

Chapter 14

MAHASAMADHI

Agroup of us quickly booked tickets and flew from Washington, D.C. to Kennedy Airport in New York, where we met about two hundred other devotees flying to India. The flight was not ideal, with three stops along the way, but it was the best we could get at such short notice. The mood was both somber and joyful. We were grieving Guruji's passing but also remembered with love and joy all he had given us. We had stops in London, Istanbul, and Dubai before we arrived at the Mumbai Airport at 2:00 a.m. Indian time. Two hundred of us lined up in the dank, humid airport corridor to pass through Indian immigration, avoiding the puddles that signaled we were still in monsoon season. At first the officials would not let us enter, saying we needed visas. Finally, one of the ashram women went to the official and cried her heart out, explaining that we had all come for Guruji's funeral. Suddenly we were all let through.

We were met by several buses that took us to Navsari. We left

Mumbai in darkness but as we neared the ashram the sun rose and an unimaginable scene spread before us. There were so many vehicles trying to get to the ashram that our bus had to stop on the road a mile away to let us out. We walked the mile uphill to the ashram through a sea of thousands of Indian devotees. Remarkably, everyone let us pass unimpeded as we slowly made our way. Guruji's burial had been held in abeyance for two days so that our large group could arrive for the ceremonies. Guruji was placed in a meditative posture on a chair in his apartment and for two days thousands of Indian devotees had filed through having their final darshan. Now it was our turn.I was moving as if in a dream. I had not slept for two days and now was in line waiting to see Guruji for the final time. The line moved quickly as the sevites hurriedly prepared for the burial ceremonies. I finally reached Guruji's chair and bowed my head to the floor, anxious to have a moment of silence with him. But before I could form a thought, I heard "MOVE," and had to quickly get up so the line could continue. Disappointment gripped my heart. My final darshan, and I had no time to offer Guruji my gratitude.

Within minutes those who had flown in had Guruji's darshan. Then Guruji was carried in his chair through the ashram to the street and onto the back of a truck that took him to Navsari for the last darshan of his guru Bapuji. Thousands of Indian devotees surrounded the truck chanting and dancing as it moved slowly toward Navsari. I was too exhausted to follow, the cacophony of the street overwhelming my senses. I stayed behind in the quiet of the ashram as sevites prepared for Guruji's burial in his original room. Standing near the door of a temple, across from the burial room, I was asked to stand guard to prevent the surge of people returning from rushing through the temple to the burial site. Glad to do seva, I stood in silence as we awaited the return of Guruji's body.

Soon the truck carrying Guruji was back, along with throngs of devotees. Guruji was carried in for his last darshan of Bapuji, whose statue stood at the far end of the temple. Guruji was then lifted toward the door where I stood guard. Unexpectedly, he now sat in his chair directly in front of me as the men carrying him tried, unsuccessfully, to move him through the doorway. Time stood still as I realized that I was facing Guruji for the last time—my true final darshan. The moment seemed to last and last. Looking into his eyes, I inwardly thanked him for all he had given me. I asked to be able to serve him in this and any other life. Finally, seeing the trouble the men were having in getting the chair through the door, I placed my hands beneath the chair and felt a surge of divine energy course through me as if I had touched Guruji's feet. With that small movement, Guruji passed through the doorway and was taken into the site for his burial.

The burial pit had been prepared ahead of time. Now Guruji was placed inside it, sitting in a meditative posture as devotees began placing all sorts of their possessions into the pit to be buried with Guruji for posterity. Brahman priests chanted mantras as a long chain of men, coated with sweat, carried buckets of dirt from outside and emptied them into the pit. It seemed to take hours, with bucket after bucket filling the burial pit, until a level and smooth surface formed on top of Guruji's shrine. The ashram grew silent as flowers were placed on top of the shrine. Devotees waved devotional lamps and final chants were sung.

The shrine room was filled with the sanyasis and several of Guruji's long-time devotees. I watched through a window as I stood just outside the shrine. Finally, Miraji, whom Guruji had announced as his successor four months previously, rose to give her final prayer for Guruji. I could see that she was shaking and distraught. No one had been closer to Guruji than Miraji. She had been raised in Guruji's presence and had spent her last five years constantly by Guruji's side as his translator and most trusted helper. I thought I was in grief over Guruji's death, but for Miraji, Guruji was the air she breathed. I looked at her and sent her as much love and support as I could. She finished her prayer, saying words Guruji had often repeated: "Rivers never drink from their own waters. Trees never eat their own fruit. He who sacrifices his body, mind, and wealth for others is a true human being. He is God walking on this earth."

With Miraji's final words, the ceremony ended. Minutes later a chant that was to go on for thirty days was started in an adjoining hall. The frenzied and chaotic activity of the morning's burial suddenly gave way to a feeling of serene peace. The ashram was once again bathed in silence and the beautiful sound of the chant spread through the ashram grounds. Deep and profound joy began to fill all of us present, despite our grief over Guruji's passing.

Later that day Miraji entered the courtyard for her first appearance as Guruji's successor. As I watched her, she seemed like a pristine jewel newly birthed into life. The image of a young chick breaking through its shell into the light of life came to my mind. Afterwards, a ceremony was held in the large *mandap*, or covered structure, to commemorate Guruji's passing and the transfer of guruhood to Miraji, followed by a five-day yajna. For days the sounds of the Vedic mantras chanted by the Brahman priests filled the ashram and mingled with the sounds of the chant still going on in the ashram courtyard. A feeling of profound bliss spread through the ashram.

In India most people are cremated at death but enlightened masters are buried because their bodies retain the merits of their spiritual attainment. Their samadhi shrines hold a vast spiritual energy that others experience when worshipping there. I remained in Navsari for thirty days after Guruji's burial, sitting daily in his samadhi shrine absorbing the divine energy. Rays of divine bliss poured unimpeded into the room. It seemed that Guruji had merged into the most rare and lofty space of divine consciousness and, for a short time, the window between that divine space and our earthly plane remained open, giving us all an experience of that divinity. Never before had I been able to sit in meditation for three hours at a time but now the energy in the shrine buoyed me. My concept of time dissolved. Merging into that divine state, I had no thoughts of grief or sorrow, only the feeling of oneness with God.

Guruji said that when an enlightened master departs from this physical plane he leaves for his disciples as much conscious spiritual energy as they can absorb. I was aware of these words during my month in Navsari and wondered what I was receiving from Guruji. In truth, it took many years for me to understand the depth of what Guruji had given me, a gift that unfolded and expanded over time. He implanted in me the experience of my own awakened heart, my divine essence, a seed that has never stopped growing, a seed whose essence was divine love. I prepared to leave Navsari feeling profoundly grateful for the eight years I spent with Guruji, one of the great spiritual masters of our time. At the same time, I could not help but feel a deep sadness that I would not be seeing his beautiful physical form again.

I was thirty-two when Guruji passed from this world. There was still much more in store for me than I could have imagined. After the ceremonies and the thirty-day chant, Shivaji and I flew back to D.C. to discover what was next for each of us.

Chapter 15

MIRAJI

My life changed, at first slowly and then dramatically, after Guruji's passing. The possibility of monkhood began to recede under Miraji's guidance. Foremost, Guruji's loss left a deep emptiness in me. Since most of his devotees were now trying to be positive about his passing, emphasizing that he was still with us on the spiritual plane, I kept my feelings to myself.

I tried to assess what I had learned from my eight years with Guruji. One of the elements Guruji taught was that spiritual practice has to be continued for a long time with sincere dedication. I had gained much from my practice and was in many ways a different person from the man who had met Guruji eight years before. Now, at my core, I was regularly aware of the divine essence within me and the knowledge that my inner nature was divine. Many of the negative thoughts and tendencies that had plagued me in my younger years were no longer part of my mental or emotional environment. I had also embraced renunciation as an essential aspect of my life, in spite of not becoming a monk. After many years of celibacy and living with few physical possessions, I felt little attraction for the worldly pleasures I assumed most people spent their lives seeking. Finally, I had devoted my life to service in Guruji's ashram and was deeply content with this choice. This impulse to be of service had become an implicit part of my identity.

Guruji had emphasized austerity, study, and surrender to God as practices leading to self- realization. These were practices I had embraced during my years with him and hoped to continue. Austerity I understood as a basic simplicity to life, leaving out what was not essential, particularly that which did not further my spiritual growth. It left me with a sense of inner freedom, not craving things I did not need. Surrender to God I understood as allowing myself to become immersed in the flow of my own inner divinity before making a decision so that I was certain my motivation was coming from a place of purity and was for the good of all. I sincerely hoped my attempts at austerity, study, and surrender to God had taken me closer to my goal of union with God.

Yet I was still a thirty-two year old man who for several years had basically removed himself from the worldly dramas that constitute the lives of most people. I had not had to earn a living for myself or support a family. I had not had to concern myself with how to spend free time, time not doing seva or spiritual practices. My daily schedule was always mapped out for me from my morning meditations to my evening chants. I had given myself to this world of monastic discipline and had learned much from it but this discipline had not been tested in the larger stage of this world.

After returning to D.C. from Guruji's mahasamadhi, I spent another year serving as the ashram manager. I did not know if I would become a monk under Miraji's guidance. In many ways I was waiting to see how life would unfold with a new guru. After a year of waiting, I requested to go to India to be with Miraji and she welcomed me there.

I arrived in India in August 1983 at the end of the monsoon season. The river near the ashram was now full and rippled through the valley. With the constant rains, it gave the sense that water was everywhere. The fields were a lush green with the villagers up to their knees in their rice paddies. It was a quiet time in the ashram. Long thick jute mats were spread through the courtyard for walking since the wet marble tiles were now slippery. There was a group of about one hundred twenty present, an unusually small number to be in the presence of the guru.

Miraji's appearance had changed significantly since I last saw her. A strong vibration of quietude now emanated from her and it appeared that she was now at peace with Guruji's passing. She had become quite beautiful and charismatic in her own unique way, distinctly different from Guruji. She sat for darshan several times a day during the monsoon as the powerful vibration of the ashram and her presence suffused us all. It was a quiet and peaceful time and I felt at home with this new expression of my spiritual life.

Being in Miraji's presence, I became conscious of how extraordinary it was that Guruji was able to pass on the power of his guruhood to Miraji. These powers are unique and remarkable. A true guru—*satguru* in Sanskrit—is able to read a person thoroughly, knowing with certainty the person's personality and lessons he or she came into this world to learn. Once a person accepts a guru and becomes a disciple, the guru's role expands to take full responsibility for guiding a disciple to spiritual maturity. Now being with Miraji, I saw her manifest these same abilities that I had witnessed so closely in Guruji.

Within a short time though, I saw that my relationship with Miraji would be quite different from the one I had with Guruji. Rather than replacing the relationship I had with Guruji, I saw that I would be forging a new and unique one with Miraji. Guruji had initiated me into the path of yoga and awakened my ability to see that within, my essence was divine. He set me on a precise path to grow spiritually that I had followed for several years. No matter what was occurring, I always felt his presence with me. Particularly in difficult times, I felt his support as if he too were sharing whatever I was experiencing. Along with being my spiritual teacher, in many ways he had been a father figure to me.

As time passed it became apparent that one of Miraji's important roles with me was to work on my ego and put me in situations, often uncomfortable, that would allow me to see more clearly the inner workings of my mind that kept me from growing spiritually. As with Guruji, I felt a deep and unconditional love coming from Miraji but she also became a strict teacher for me. The great fifteenth century poet and spiritual master Kabir likened a guru to a potter who beats the clay on the outside to give it its necessary shape while supporting it from within so the work can be done. This aptly describes how I experienced Miraji working on me.

On coming to Navsari, my desire was to again become a permanent sevite in the ashram. But shortly after I arrived, Miraji instructed me to stay for only four months. This sent me into a mental tailspin and brought up intense feelings of being unappreciated. For the first time, I sincerely contemplated leaving the ashram. I pictured myself using my intellect, which I thought had long been lying dormant, and working as a lawyer, helping others and being thanked for it. For three months I wallowed in negative thoughts and feelings. Then suddenly everything changed. One day Miraji approached and told me that I could stay in the ashram. Soon I was assigned a seva that had me working from early morning late into the night. I relished the chance to serve again and dove wholeheartedly into my seva. Once more I felt an integral part of the ashram.

One night, about 10:00 p.m., soon after falling asleep, I was awakened by a messenger with an emergency. One of the ashram women had to leave early the next morning due to an illness in her family and needed an exit permit from the Navsari police before she could legally depart India. I jumped on my old, functional bicycle and rode the mile into town along the rutted half-paved road in the dark. Most of the town was asleep but I saw a light in the police station and inside an officer was sitting at his desk. After I explained what I needed, he told me the police chief was at a party and would be back later. I sat for over an hour waiting for the chief to return. Finally I hired a taxi to take me to the neighboring town where the party was. It was after midnight when I found the chief and convinced him to leave the party and return to the station with me.

It was a bizarre scene at the police station. The chief was sitting at his desk, annoyed at being taken from his party. A single bulb lit the room with a fog of flies and mosquitoes surrounding it. It was still extremely hot at this late hour. The chief was noticeably intoxicated and irritated at being called back to work. Finally, he said, "Give me a camera from America and some t-shirts and I'll write out the exit permit for you." It was now past 1:00 a.m. I was tired and annoyed that the chief was asking for a bribe. Looking directly in his eyes, I told him that it would be better if he just did his job and gave me the permit. This did not sit well with him and he squirmed in his seat, looking uncomfortable. Finally he relented, gave me the permit, and I returned to the ashram.

The next morning the ashram managers congratulated me for getting the exit permit. They were pleased that the woman was able to make her flight. Soon after Miraji noticed me in the courtyard and called me over. Smiling, she said, "You should give all of your seva to Dan," one of my close friends. I was in shock. Suddenly I was losing the seva that I loved. I had told no one about my experience with the police chief the night before but concluded that Miraji was responding to how I had embarrassed him. Although she spoke to me without harshness or blame, I felt I had somehow failed in my interaction with him.

Soon after my funds for remaining in India ran out. I asked Miraji if I could return to the D.C. ashram to earn some money. She was scheduled to visit D.C. the next month to give public programs so she told me to return there, find a job, and wait for her. I had spent eight months with Miraji in Navsari with no mention of sanyasa. I now wondered what direction my spiritual life would take. Leaving

India feeling confused and conflicted, I had no idea what Miraji had in store for me.

In late May 1984, I returned to the D.C. ashram and was warmly greeted by my friends in the community. I told the new ashram manager about Miraji's instructions for me and started to look for a job. However, the manager was anxious about the large amount of preparation around Miraji's arrival and asked me to oversee the financial seva for her visit. He said I could find a job later. At first I refused, wanting to follow Miraji's instructions, but eventually acquiesced, seeing how desperate he was for my help. A few weeks later, Miraji arrived. When she discovered I was doing financial seva, she immediately told me to leave the ashram and find a job.

A few days later, on her final day in D.C., Miraji held a meeting at the ashram. About one hundred devotees from the community were invited. At the meeting she called me up in front of everyone and asked if I had found a job yet. When I answered no, she looked at me with what I took to be intense disapproval and said, "You should find a job and earn your living with the sweat of your own blood. And you should learn a skill." I was in shock. I looked around at the faces of the community members who had known and loved me as their ashram manager. Few could meet my gaze. I wondered what I had done wrong. Feeling the foundation of my spiritual life slipping away, I wondered what I would do after having devoted my past ten years to ashram life.

Chapter 16

LAW

I had no choice but to leap into the process of finding a job and a place to live. I also had to decide what skill I wanted to learn for the next stage in my life. Too upset to clearly contemplate what had just happened, I put my energy into dealing with the practical necessities I now faced.

From my youth I had long admired the lawyers who played crucial roles in the U.S. civil rights movement. Law had always seemed a worthy profession to me, a profession where I could be of service to others. Recalling my reading with Rosemarie years before, I considered the field of immigration law. I weighed my options for enrolling in law school but knew it would take me two years to finish my bachelor's degree and another three to finish law school. I was not ready for that kind of commitment. Instead I enrolled in a year-long paralegal program at Georgetown University. At the same time, I found a job in a small law firm as office manager, bookkeeper, and paralegal.

Suddenly my life appeared quite different than it had been. I was now living in a spacious apartment with a friend off Rock Creek Park, in Northwest Washington, D.C. I had an older but dependable car, was working in a law firm during the days, and going to school at night. It was a hectic schedule but, in reality, I continued to live like a monk. Each morning I arose early before work, meditated, and chanted. Each evening before bed I again meditated, read from my spiritual books, and contemplated the changes that had occurred in my life. I was now a monk hidden in the world.

I found working in a law firm surprisingly simple after my many years of seva. In the ashram an internal process was always occurring, requiring attention and mindfulness to whatever I was doing. It was not always easy. I realized that, even when I rested in the ashram, a deep inner work took place. Now, at the law firm, I found the only thing expected of me was to do a competent job. This was not difficult at all.

The owner of the law firm was an intelligent, soft-spoken man who, from the start, was pleased with my work. It was easy relating to him and the other attorneys. I spent a lot of time at the local courthouses, delivering papers, or visiting the law libraries at nearby law schools, doing research or finding cases for the associate attorneys. It was easy and relaxed and I found the work interesting. I also found the classes at Georgetown more interesting than I expected and started making friends with some of my classmates.

As the year progressed, I became reasonably content with my new life. But in the back of my mind there was always the hope that I would return to the ashram. I waited patiently as my work and studies continued, knowing that after receiving my paralegal certificate, I would ask Miraji if I could return.

Near the end of the year, a member of our community invited me to his wedding party. I had not been to a party of this sort for many years, with wine and drinks, music, and dancing. Many of my friends from the community were there. I sat next to an attractive young woman who I liked and found interesting. We had a fun evening sharing stories and dancing. I had forgotten how much I liked to dance. At the end of the party, a slow song was played and I asked her to dance. It had been a long time since I had held a woman in my arms and it awoke long-lost feelings in me. It was a part of my life I had cherished when I was younger, before my ashram days. I realized that a part of me still longed for this even though I was still committed to becoming a monk. It was the final dance of the evening and the party was soon over. I made sure to have the woman's phone number before we parted. I was interested in seeing her again.

I spent many agonizing nights trying to decide what to do about this woman. I knew that if I called and asked her out we would fall into a relationship. I could tell she liked me as much as I her. But I still had a dream of becoming a monk. I still wanted to devote my life to God. Night after night I lay in bed wondering if I should call this woman and ask her out. Each night I painfully decided I would not. It was difficult to go through and I did not share it with anyone. Slowly, after several weeks, she began to recede from my mind.

Finally, after a year of work and study, having earned my paralegal certificate, I received a message from Miraji to return to Navsari. I was immensely happy. My life was still dedicated to service and spiritual growth and I yearned to be back in the environment that most supported this. Yet I had learned much from my year in the world. I appreciated the skills I had learned and the people I had met. It had been a truly beautiful year.

Chapter 17

RETURN TO NAVSARI

I flew back to India in September 1985. It was still hot, rainy, and humid from the monsoons and the lands surrounding the ashram were lush with tropical growth. I noted how well I felt when I arrived. I felt strong and self-confident after my year in the world.

Within days of arriving, I was posted back to the previous seva from the year before. Then, in October, Miraji left Navsari to begin a teaching tour in the U.S. By the end of October the ashram was again quiet, the population having shrunk to eighty. Instead of being surrounded by intense activity and crowds, I found myself in a quiet, monastic space. The silent, powerful vibration of the ashram was more palpable than ever. I now focused more on the practices of meditation, chanting, and study than on seva. I became close with the others staying behind and slowly settled into a peaceful, monastic life.

During this time I became intimate with the unique sense of

the land surrounding the ashram, its people, its vegetation and fragrances, and the steady flow of its seasons. Some days I hiked to a reservoir hidden in the mountains nearby, a good hour's walk through a forested area that was sparsely populated, where I swam in the cool, pure water. There were also small towns farther down the road from the ashram situated near the river, which had hot springs. In the cooler weather, I rode my bike out to these more remote areas. The simplicity and stark beauty of the land fascinated me. In contrast the poverty and lack of education of the villagers was difficult to observe. My ashram days were filled with meditation, chanting, and seva. The cooler weather brought a welcome relief as we gathered in the early morning hours before sunrise, our shawls wrapped around us, to meditate and chant. A deep inner joy suffused the ashram and I marveled at how fortunate I was to be there.

After a few months, I allowed myself to become attracted to a petite, young ashram woman from the States named Sarah. I began to spend time with her at meals and after dinner. Acutely recalling my aborted non-relationship in D.C., I wondered if I could drop my reservations and take steps toward a relationship with Sarah.

Sarah was living alone in a large room in one of the dormitory buildings, which afforded us a measure of privacy as we took small steps toward our relationship. One evening, after spending time with her for several weeks, I became aware that we had carried on past the point of retreating. Sitting near her, with a mixture of wonder and disbelief, I moved closer, put my arms around her, and kissed her. It had been eleven years since I had kissed a woman and it awoke in me all the feelings an aspiring monk chooses not to experience.

That night after dinner Sarah and I walked into the town of Navsari and rented a room in a guesthouse, where we removed our clothes and made love. It was blissful and tender. Had it been this way before? I was not sure I could remember but I was surely a different person than the lad who had romanced Anne in Paris. I was now older and had the divine light of my spiritual practices flowing through me. My sexuality still shared many of the attributes

I experienced in my younger years but was now tempered by my years of spiritual practice.

After returning to the ashram a few hours later, I found myself wandering through its dark, quiet pathways thinking about what had just occurred. Alone in the still atmosphere, I contemplated the ending of my celibacy and, most likely, my attempt to become a monk. I could not yet grasp the implications of my choice but I sensed that it had been inevitable. I was moving from the role of a monk to something else and the process was pulling me along with it.

Soon after Miraji sent a video to those of us doing seva in Navsari in which she spoke about not judging the actions of others. She said, at the end of her talk, "Some people choose to break their celibacy after eleven years. We should not judge them for that." From these words I surmised that Miraji was well aware of what was happening to me and was not in disapproval.

Sarah and I continued our relationship for a few months but I gradually began to feel that we were not a good couple. We did not share the same goals nor were our interests fully harmonious. Still, there was a strong bond created by our sexual liaison that was hard for me to give up. I did not know how to peaceably extricate myself from the relationship or if I truly wanted to.

I wrote to Miraji and told her of my feelings. She wrote back that if I was not committed to marrying Sarah it was best for me to end the relationship. Sarah was then recalled to the New York ashram while I remained in Navsari. For a few months, I was emotionally raw and tender. Even though I did not want to proceed with Sarah I still missed her company. For a time I wondered if I had made the right decision. My affair with Sarah left me disturbed and confused, feeling I had gone out on a limb, relinquishing my ability to become a monk but also failing to find a fulfilling relationship.

In September Miraji returned to the ashram. She immediately noticed my ambivalent state of mind and began working on me. First she removed me from the seva I was doing, in which I saw myself as a key part of the functioning of the ashram. Then she assigned me to the dish room, a grueling seva in which I washed dishes several hours per day in the scorching heat. I gamely tried not to take it as a punishment. As the days rolled by I became more despondent. One afternoon I approached Miraji. I told her how difficult it was when she was so hard on me. Almost pleading, I said I needed to feel more love from her. She was quiet for a moment and then responded simply, "Love yourself first."

Yes, that was the problem. I was floundering and discouraged because of my failed relationship with Sarah. Moreover, I was no longer clear about the direction of my spiritual life or my place in the ashram. No longer an aspiring monk, I was also reluctant to try another relationship. I felt stuck and angry. I felt that Miraji was only making things worse by taking me out of seva I felt comfortable and secure in. Seeing my inner turmoil, Miraji said, "It takes a thorn to remove another thorn. I'm removing your negativity with my negativity." A few days later, she told me it was time to leave Navsari.

I had been the recipient of Miraji's strict discipline several times but for once was not overwhelmed by it. I was clearly in a despondent state and needed a push to get my bearings. Although Miraji appeared harsh, I felt the love beneath her words and knew she was acting for my welfare. Collecting myself, I prepared to depart Navsari after my eighteen-month stay, my longest in this most wonderful of places.

On a night in late December, I was driven to the airport by an Australian swami who had lived in India for many years and spoke fluent Hindi. On the way we stopped off the main road to find a simple teashop. The swami told me it had the best chai in Mumbai. We each enjoyed steaming glasses of hot chai as I contemplated the events of the past months. Realizing it was my last chai in India and my last conversation with a fellow devotee before embarking on the next phase of my life, I silently offered thanks for my deep experiences in India and hoped I might again return to this place of awe and wonder.

Chapter 18

TRANSITION

Within a month I was working in a prestigious product liability law firm in downtown New York City. The office was plush and took up the whole forty-first floor of an elegant office building overlooking the Hudson and East Rivers as they merged below the tip of lower Manhattan. It was a remarkable change from the rice paddies and mud huts of Navsari but was not a difficult transition. Again the simple duty of just doing a good job seemed incredibly easy compared to the constant inner work that occurred in the ashram. I enjoyed the people I worked with but found the paralegal work unchallenging. There was a strict line between what a paralegal and a lawyer could do and within months I had reached the peak of my responsibilities. Nonetheless, I was making more money than I ever had and started to save what funds I could.

After eighteen months I was at my wits' end with the limitations of my job and started looking for more interesting work. One afternoon I found a listing for a position at an immigration law firm. Ever since my reading with Rosemarie several years before, I had been interested in immigration law. I called the office and was told to come over immediately for an interview.

The office was in the Woolworth Building, a one-hundred-story landmark building in Lower Manhattan, once the tallest building in the city. I took the elevator up to the thirty-third floor and entered an office that was old-fashioned and threadbare. It had obviously not been remodeled for many years. It reminded me of the offices in Mumbai I had visited for my sevas in India. Ironically, the man who welcomed me was an elderly Indian man from Mumbai who held an undefined role in the firm. The attorney turned out to be an experienced and well-known immigration lawyer, a brilliant but eccentric man who was also familiar with yoga and meditation. When he saw on my resume that I had spent several years in an ashram, he hired me on the spot. I was to start as soon as possible.

The law firm was more unorganized than what I was used to. No longer working in a cushy, manicured office doing low-level administrative work, I was now in a rather unkempt office but in a position to directly help immigrants from a wide variety of backgrounds. I volunteered to take on as much work as I could and, for a change, my position as a paralegal did not create a barrier. I had an immediate affinity to immigration law and was soon seeing several clients a day, doing my best to help them with their issues. As time passed I felt more comfortable in this setting and began to feel that I had found my niche in the legal field.

Then, in February 1990, after working at the firm for two years, I received a letter from Miraji inviting me to come to Navsari for a year. I was to come as soon as possible. At first I was startled by the invitation and wondered if Miraji knew how well I was doing in my new role. But soon I became excited about returning to Navsari and started making plans for my trip. Knowing my employer would have a hard time finding a replacement for me, I gave him four months notice. In June 1990 I was ready to return to India.

I arrived in Navsari in late June, this time at the start of the monsoon season and just in time for Miraji's birthday celebrations. When Miraji saw me, she exclaimed in front of an exited group, "The old man's back!" Everyone broke into laughter. For a week there was much discussion about where I would offer seva. I was placed in an office that oversaw legal issues regarding how the ashram purchased certain types of goods. I was told repeatedly how important this seva was. It took me a couple of weeks to fully grasp the intricate laws behind the work but soon afterwards I realized that there was little work to do. I often sat in the office for hours a day without really doing anything. At one point I went to Miraji and asked if I could help with another seva. She responded that I was far too busy.

Some weeks later the ashram manager asked if I would help doing construction purchasing in my spare time. I of course agreed. The ashram was constantly expanding and engaged in a variety of construction projects including several in the surrounding villages as part of its charitable work. My role was to ride into Mumbai three times a week to purchase construction supplies from the vendors in Mumbai's Nagdevi district. It seemed simple enough.

Having been accustomed to working in a law office the past two years, I found that I was not prepared for the physically grueling nature of the purchasing seva. I left early each morning at 6:00 a.m., before sunrise, on a van with other sevites. The road to Mumbai at the time was a narrow, two-lane affair crammed with trucks spewing out black fumes of exhaust with no discernible mechanisms to filter out the pollution. Since the van had an air conditioning unit that rarely worked, and because it was normally very hot, we drove with the windows open and breathed in the polluted air for the whole two and a half hour trip. I arrived in Mumbai coated with dust from the road, my lungs aching and my shirt plastered to my body with sweat. Ironically, I then entered one of the city's most posh hotels for breakfast, looking like I had just run a marathon in my clothes. The breakfast in the clean, air-conditioned and quiet atmosphere of the hotel allowed me to recoup my energies for the work ahead.

I then took a taxi to the Nagdevi district where vendors of all sorts of construction materials had their offices. The streets in the area were unpaved and deeply rutted, filled with bone-thin laborers pulling heavily laden, two-wheel carts through the busy throngs. It seemed a scene from an ancient slave culture. The vendors were friendly and often invited me into their offices for tea as I bargained with them on prices for their goods. It normally took several hours to complete my rounds. At the end of the day, I went to a local pool to swim and wash off the grit from the day's work. At 5:00 p.m. the van left from Mumbai and we returned to the ashram about 7:30 p.m.

I never liked to complain about seva but I found this one mentally draining and physically exhausting. As a result, for the next two months I was not in a good frame of mind. I found my seva an act of endurance rather than an eager offering of selfless service. However, one evening, while giving a talk, Miraji related having to go into Mumbai for some dental work. She said that when she saw how difficult the trip was she thought of the sevites who regularly made the trip. She stated that her heart went out to them and then, incredibly, said, "I give them half of my merits."

In the eastern religions, it is believed that when people perform good actions, those that benefit others or spread love in this world, they accrue merits, or good karma, that goes with them when they leave this world. These merits help them in this life and in lives to come. I could only imagine what Miraji's merits were, since her life was devoted to serving and uplifting others on a grand scale. I had never read of someone transferring merits to another and wondered what Miraji meant by her words, whether she was being metaphorical or literal. Whatever Miraji's intent, my attitude toward my seva abruptly changed. I began to perceive it as a gift to be doing this difficult work and started to appreciate and enjoy my long hours on the streets of Mumbai.

In October 1990 the ninth and final large celebration for Guruji's mahasamadhi was held. As in previous years, a yajna took place and also a five-day chant. Tens of thousands came from all over India and the world to take part. Huge tents were set up to house and feed the thousands who came.

The celebrations culminated with the finale of the five-day chant held in the ashram courtyard. Surprising everyone, instead of ending the chant at the ashram, Miraji took to the street outside the ashram and led the chant all the way to the town of Navsari to the samadhi shrine of Bapuji. Thousands followed Miraji down the road chanting and dancing with her on their way to the shrine. The samadhi shrine was quickly packed to capacity, with a huge overflow onto the streets. The chanting continued as Miraji had the darshan of the statue of Bapuji in his samadhi shrine.

At one point I left the samadhi shrine and went around to the back to sit on a stone ledge in relative quiet, overcome by the emotion of the event. Soon I heard the chant had ended and saw many people make their way back to the ashram. Sitting in the solitary back courtyard, I saw the back door to the shrine open and Miraji walk out, swaying in the intoxication of her divine state. As I watched her, I felt waves of divine energy emanating from her. I wondered what she was feeling in this moment. What could it possibly feel like to embody the full power of guruhood, the power to transmit a divine spiritual awareness into seekers and awaken their ability to evolve meaningfully on the spiritual path? For a moment our eyes locked and the divine energy emanating from her flowed even more powerfully into me, putting me into a state of *samadhi*. I was left in awe at this divine transmission. Miraji then turned from me to return to the ashram. I was unable to move for some time. Sitting there, I felt it was really for this experience that Miraji had invited me back to India. Something intangible and profound had occurred for me with this transmission. I intuited that I had just completed a profound cycle of my spiritual journey. Feelings of deep gratitude swept through me.

I stayed in India for a year before returning to the New York ashram to help create a new visa department. I did not know it at the time but it was my last trip to Navsari. One afternoon in the

New York ashram I was in the lobby when Miraji appeared. She turned her gaze toward me and looked at me for several seconds in her penetrating way. At once the familiar feeling of working in the world swept through me. I knew instantly that Miraji was sending me a message: it was time for me to work again. That night I wrote to her, thanking her for my year in India and asking permission to leave the ashram and go back to work. Unexpectedly, at the end of the letter, I wrote, "And I would like to go to law school." I was not sure where the words came from but as they came out I knew without doubt I would be going to law school. Days later I received a message from Miraji giving her blessings for my new endeavor.

Part III

The Journey Home

Chapter 19

MARRIAGE

It was November 1991, chilly and windy in Manhattan. My friend Arnie let me use his apartment and phone for the day—there were no cell phones—and I tried to hustle up a job for myself. I was starting over again with no money but I was used to this and knew I would be able to find work. I had a directory of immigration lawyers in the city and started with the A's. A quarter of the way through I found an attorney interested in my skills and within days had a job as an immigration paralegal.

Next I rented a studio apartment on the Upper West Side. It was tiny but nicely appointed, in a newly renovated building. Since I had few possessions the size did not matter much. It felt great to have the privacy of my own space. I paid the first month's rent and security deposit with a credit card and moved in the next day. With a place to live and a job under my belt, I started looking for a way to complete my bachelor's degree. This was not easy since I lacked three semesters of courses to complete my degree. Luckily, the State of New York had a college designed for older students who had accumulated significant life and work experience. Located in Albany, it agreed to grant me a year's worth of credits in Eastern Religious Studies based on my studies in the ashram and a semester's worth of credit for my studies and experience as a paralegal, conditioned on my passing oral exams with professors in these fields. For two full days I appeared at the college, meeting with professors of Eastern Religions and Law, where I expounded on what I had learned and answered their questions. The religion professors became intensely interested in what I had learned in a non-academic environment. They couldn't keep from enthusiastically asking questions about areas they had not yet explored. Both later came to the New York ashram with me to meet Miraji. In May 1992 I completed my credits and earned my bachelor's degree. I had started in 1966. Soon after I was admitted to a night program at Fordham Law School. Classes met Monday through Thursday from 6:00 p.m. to 9:15 p.m. Within ten months of leaving the ashram, I was working in the field I loved, had completed my bachelor's degree, and had enrolled in law school. Three months later I met the woman who would become my wife.

During my stay at Navsari the year before, while taking part in a program, I had listened to one of the teachers tell a story. It was about a man who left home at an early age knowing he would never be able to see his mother again. He knew how hard this would be on his mother but he was called to leave home. When I heard the story, I thought of Guruji, who left his home at fifteen to become a monk and never again saw his mother. As I thought this, Miraji turned and looked directly at me. Recognition suddenly hit me. Yes, I too had left my mother at a rather early age to go to college. And I hadn't been able to spend much time with her after that, traveling around the world as a hippie and then living in an ashram. I realized how hard this had been for my mother and felt great remorse. When she died in 1982, a few months before Guruji passed away, her last wish for me was to have a wife and family. Now, this story mysteriously awakened deep feelings within me and I knew without doubt that it was time for me to find a wife.

Entering law school and living alone, I began to actively seek a partner. In late December at a party at a friend's apartment in Manhattan I met Patricia, a pretty woman in her early thirties, to whom I was immediately attracted. We spent most of the evening talking and at the end of the party I walked her home. We lived only a block away. That evening we spoke for a long time, both of us aware of how comfortable we were with each other. The next evening we had dinner at a local restaurant.

We met each evening that week after my classes. As we became closer we each shared our fears of entering a relationship. I felt awkward with women after living so many years as a monk. Patricia had fears from her childhood that were preventing her from being open to a relationship. We decided that we would at least be friends and help each other in working out our fears. From this agreement a deep trust arose between us and whatever barriers existed quickly fell away. Suddenly I was again in a relationship with a woman and this time it felt right. Within a short time, we were inseparable.

Soon after meeting Patricia and I went to the ashram to visit Miraji. Seeing us together, Miraji laughed and placed her forefingers together in the sign of a couple, saying, "You are together?" When we said yes, she made a joyful gesture of approval. Then she turned to us and said, "So, you found each other." But Miraji could not help playing with me. On one of our visits, she asked humorously in front of a group, "How did you find such a good wife, bald skinny guy like you?"

Within weeks I found myself reveling in a truly intimate relationship. In our spare time, Patricia and I roamed the Upper West Side, frequenting coffee houses and restaurants and taking long walks through Central Park. We stayed up late together every night, relishing our new intimacy. As I got to know her better, I asked her if she wanted me to teach her some of the Indian philosophies I had studied. Without hesitating, she said no. She was not interested in having me as her teacher. She simply wanted someone to love who loved her in return.

After a few months, I moved into Patricia's apartment and we began planning our wedding. Initially I had envisioned us living in the ashram together after I finished law school, with both of us dedicated to spiritual life. However, I soon saw that this would not happen. Patricia wanted a family life and children, things I had never considered. Also, the debt I was accumulating from law school would take a long time to pay off. I could not pay it off living in the ashram. With a surprising suddenness, I realized that my ashram days were over. This caused me a considerable amount of grief.

As my relationship with Patricia continued to grow, the intense schedule I had undertaken began to take a toll on me. I woke early each morning to do my meditation, worked as a paralegal during the day, and then went to law school in the evenings. Afterwards, I had dinner at a nearby restaurant and then spent a couple of hours with Patricia. Finally, I studied my law texts. I never got to bed before 1:00 a.m. Toward the end of my first year of law school, I began to show symptoms of chronic fatigue. I am sure that my ambivalence about breaking with my ashram life played a factor in my illness. I loved my ashram life and was heartbroken to let go of it. But I was acutely aware that the path I was choosing with Patricia was the direction I needed to follow.

In the 90s doctors were not familiar with chronic fatigue and most did not know how to diagnose or treat it. I saw several doctors who assured me that there was nothing wrong with me and that my problems were mental. Some advised me to drink more coffee. Mental or not, I did have chronic fatigue and it took me more than a year to get over the worst symptoms.

After completing my finals, Patricia and I moved into a roomy apartment in Tarrytown, north of the city in Westchester County. It was surrounded by trees and near the Hudson River and several parks. It was a welcome change. Still ill, I skipped my next year of law school as I slowly recovered. I commuted into Manhattan three days a week for a few hours of work at an immigration firm but that was the most I could handle. Gradually, my strength returned.

At one point I consulted a doctor who I had known in the ashram. I was at first reluctant to seek his advice since he was a rather traditional physician and I had not had much luck with physicians. Still, I met with him and he offered advice that changed my life. He pointed out that I had taken on too much, with law school, work, and now my relationship with Patricia, and that I needed to simplify my life. New York was the most stressful environment to live and work that he could imagine. He suggested I pick a simpler and more beautiful place to live where I could finish law school and enjoy my life. With his words a great weight was lifted from me.

With excitement, Patricia and I started planning our move, enthused about finding a beautiful place to live and set up our home. We considered several places but decided on Gainesville, Florida, a small but beautiful town in northern Florida where I could resume my studies at the University of Florida Law School.

In April of 1994, Patricia and I were married in the ballroom of the Convent of the Sacred Heart in New York City. Many of our ashram friends attended as well as other friends and family members. The next month we moved to Gainesville, where our new life began.

Chapter 20

FAMILY AND LAW

Late one afternoon, a rainy day in March 1995, Patricia's contractions began. We jumped into our old red Ford Tempo and drove to the birthing center. The midwife examined Patricia and then dismissed us, saying we were too early and that the birth would not happen for a while. We returned home where immediately Patricia's water broke. We quickly made our way back to the birthing center. I prepared by bringing a tape deck with some yoga chanting, incense, and a candle to make a peaceful, serene environment for the birth. But giving birth is not peaceful or serene. Patricia started having strong contractions when we arrived and I sat and watched as nature took its course. Finally, just before midnight, a beautiful girl, Anna, was born, barely crying. The midwife saw that Anna had some fluid in her lungs so we hopped into her Volkswagon bug and went to the hospital across the street. Patricia needed stitches before she could join us.

There I was in the back of an old Volkswagen, holding my little daughter Anna in my arms, feeling enchanted and full of love. We entered the hospital where she was put in an incubator for a short time while her lungs cleared. I sat by her side. She seemed a remarkable baby, quiet and self-absorbed. She reminded me of a Tibetan Buddhist monk. Her skin was tinted red from her birth, similar to the color of the robes of a Tibetan monk, and her hair was remarkably short and black. I was grateful for the chance to be with her so soon after her birth. Soon Patricia arrived and started to feed Anna. The three of us slept together in the hospital that night.

The next morning we drove home in a light rain, three of us now. As young as she was, I saw right away that Anna was a person in her own right, an equal among equals. Our family life had begun.

Our apartment in Gainesville was surrounded by greenery with large live oak trees forming a magnificent canopy over the sprawling apartment complex. The gardens sported an amazing variety of plants: azaleas in March, gardenias in May, and crepe myrtles in June. It was luxurious after being in New York and I found law school surprisingly undemanding compared to my frantic life in the city.

I still had not fully recovered from my chronic fatigue, although I now had the energy to attend classes, do my studying, work remotely a few hours a week for a lawyer in New York, and be a father. Not having luck with traditional doctors, I sought out alternative healing sources to see why I hadn't fully recovered my energy: acupuncture, reiki, and a variety of chiropractors. They seemed to help but only in a limited way.

I then discovered a group of healers from rural Virginia who made flower essence remedies with the assistance of disincarnate beings from a higher plane. When I took the essences, I was instantly aware of their high vibration and healing properties. The group offered another more esoteric healing modality with these disincarnate beings, which I decided to try. One evening, following their written instructions, I lay down on a futon and invited these beings to heal me, describing through my thoughts what my health problems were. I soon felt their presence and experienced waves of energy going through my body as they worked on me. The session lasted forty-five minutes and I came out of it feeling balanced and remarkably lightened. I continued with these sessions weekly for several months and my health dramatically improved. It seemed my body had become extremely sensitive from my years in the ashram and I was especially receptive to healing techniques arising from these high, more refined vibrations.

I completed my law degree in 1996, having enjoyed law school and the daily give-and-take with several of the professors with whom I had became friends. Soon after graduating I opened a law practice in Gainesville and within months my son Jonathan was born. Within four years of leaving New York, I had a family of four, a law practice, and a home in a beautiful tree-lined neighborhood in Gainesville.

My law practice grew quickly. Just months after opening my practice, the attorney with the largest immigration practice in town offered to sell me his firm. Suddenly I had the largest immigration practice in the region and was attracting clients from a broad area that was conspicuously lacking in immigration lawyers. My practice expanded exponentially. I remembered Rosemarie's words to me in the 70s: "I see you working with immigrants who have nowhere else to turn." The vision was becoming a reality.

In 1998 Congress passed a law that enabled immigrants illegally in the U.S. to proceed through a process that would legalize their status. I was uniquely positioned to help these immigrants and they came to me in numbers I could barely handle. The area surrounding Gainesville was rural farmland with a variety of agricultural businesses that depended on Mexican and Central American labor: growers, dairies, horse farms, pine straw farms, and so on. I found that I was the only immigration lawyer in the area working with these businesses and their workers.

We were able to legalize hundreds of immigrants during those few years, giving me a sense of accomplishment and making my firm very successful. As a result I was now earning more than I ever could have imagined. It was a new experience for me. I had been content for many years living out of a suitcase and trunk during my ashram years. Now I was able to provide things for my family I never considered possible before. I felt fortunate. I looked back on my time with Guruji when he had me work outside the ashram to pay for my room and board and intuited the connection between his guidance and my new prosperity. In the spiritual tradition of India, one always brings an offering to one's guru, however small, in return for the guidance, support, and grace the guru offers. Now I saw that Guruji's guidance, having me take as little materially from the ashram as possible, allowed me to attract abundance later in my life when it was really needed.

The most difficult part of my practice was being present in immigration court representing clients the government was trying to deport. Although I found that the judges were fair and impartial, the atmosphere at the courts was intense. I was acutely aware of the fear that seemed to permeate the walls of the courtrooms. Moreover, the caseload for the judges and government attorneys was overwhelming, creating additional pressure on them that often, in my opinion, led to errors.

I was surprisingly successful in the immigration court setting but the few cases I lost weighed heavily on me. Then, by 2007, I was no longer able to help many of the immigrants coming to me because the legal pathways allowing for their legalization had expired. Now I had to inform them that there was nothing I could do. At best, I could position them to take advantage of new legislation that seemed to be on the horizon. However, in 2007 and 2008, two promising laws before Congress did not pass and my clients were left with no legal pathways.

In 2008, traveling with my family in New Mexico, I met a Native American shaman. Distressed about my clients, I asked her for a reading. She said she saw many of my clients lighting candles for me at night, praying that I could help them. They were depending on me and saw me as their protector. She urged me to do as much as I could for them. I was well aware of how much my clients depended on me but hearing this did little to relieve my stress. In fact it made it worse. I felt deeply responsible for my clients and despaired when I was not able to help them more.

Chapter 21

HEALING

The courtroom at the immigration court was dreary, dark, and almost always cold. It had a Kafkaesque feeling due to the Byzantine immigration laws and practices that immigrants were subject to. My client was a Mexican man in his mid-twenties who had been in the States since he was a child. I had been able to win cases for his sisters but his was more complicated because of several arrests when he was younger. His case had already lasted over four years as we resolved some of his prior arrests. We were looking forward to his hearing since many of the hurdles that kept him from legalizing his situation had finally been overcome.

Then, two months before his hearing, his wife, an American woman from rural Florida, uneducated and suffering from depression, got into an argument with a relative in their home and called the police. The relative was also an illegal Mexican. When the police arrived, the wife apologized for calling them and said she did not wish to press charges. The police, however, were annoyed that they had been called to this home without being able to make an arrest and told them they had to arrest someone. So my client, protecting his relative, allowed himself to be arrested. His court-appointed attorney had him plead guilty to simple battery, an offense that was clearly non-deportable.

We appeared before an open-minded, respectful immigration judge I had been before many times. Almost immediately the Immigration and Customs Enforcement attorney argued that my client's arrest made him deportable, although case law clearly said it did not. The judge did not agree with my legal arguments and ordered my client deported. I was appalled he was making such an obvious mistake. I appealed the case to the Board of Immigration Appeals in Washington, DC. I had already won one such appeal in the case and it had taken over two years for the board to make its decision. I knew that with this appeal my client would remain in a legal limbo for another two years. Eventually the board approved my second appeal, almost three years later. It then took over another year for my client to finally win his case before the judge.

This type of occurrence was not unusual in my practice and was making my job more stressful. Symptoms of chronic fatigue began to reappear. I contacted an old friend, a noted astrologer, to gain some insight into my situation. Usually when I was going through a difficult time I would discover that I was in the midst of a Saturn transit. After I told her of my health issues, my astrologer said she had just returned from Brazil, where a spiritual healer cured her of a serious heart ailment. She described the healer in glowing terms as well as the environment in which the healings took place. She went on to say that my astrological chart showed me traveling to Latin America sometime in the near future. The healer was called John of God. He was a medium who channeled disincarnate beings from a higher plane. These beings performed healings that often seemed miraculous.

I was skeptical about getting involved with a medium. It seemed outside the scope of the spirituality I had practiced for years. Still, I respected my friend and read the book she suggested about John of God. When I first opened the book, before even reading the introduction, I felt a stream of white light enter my crown chakra and spread throughout my body. A feeling of deep love pervaded me for several hours. Astonished and intrigued, I went on to read a moving account of the spiritual healings performed by John of God. It reminded me of my sessions with the flower essence healers years before. I decided to visit John of God and see if his healings would have a beneficial effect on me.

I flew to Brazil in February 2007. There I discovered the Casa de Dom Inacio, the healing center of John of God, in the small town of Abadiania. John was given the name John of God by others. He referred to himself simply as Joao or Joao Medium. For three days a week, he held sessions at the Casa in which he left his body and allowed a series of entities to enter and perform healings. It sounded strange to me but as I sat in the Casa environment I instinctively felt these entities were very powerful and spiritually pure. Long attuned to the pure vibrations of the ashram, I had faith that the entities performing the healings were beneficial and trustworthy.

The town of Abadiania was an hour-and-a-half ride south of the capital Brasilia in a remote, rural area of southern Brazil. The Casa was the center of the town. Around it sprang several *pousadas*, hotels that supported the work of John of God. Most of the pousadas were simple, open-air structures that offered three nourishing meals per day and clean rooms where visitors rested and recuperated from their healings. My pousada was filled with beautiful gardens. Its walkways were surrounded by tropical flowering plants native to southern Brazil. It was a simple but beautiful environment, extremely supportive for healing. The Casa itself was also a simple structure constructed over a massive bed of crystal. It encompassed an open-air great hall and smaller meditation rooms inside.

The proprietor of my pousada was a long-time friend of John of God and guided me through the necessary steps for my healings.

Arriving at the Casa early Wednesday morning to find a seat in the main hall, I sat for an hour meditating in the spiritually-charged atmosphere. Finally, John arrived and walked to a platform at the front of the hall where two of his assistants held onto his arms. In a moment he had left his body and one of the entities had incorporated. The change in his appearance was acutely noticeable. Soon the incorporated entity went into one of the inner rooms and sat in a chair as lines of people approached him with their medical problems.

As I approached John of God, I wanted to look him in the eyes to discern what type of being he was. This proved difficult as he avoided my gaze and said offhandedly, "Spiritual surgery this afternoon." Trusting the process, I returned that afternoon for my spiritual surgery. I again waited in line to see John of God and was led to a smaller room where about forty-five people were sitting on rows of benches waiting to have their spiritual surgeries. We were told to place our right hands either on the area of our bodies that needed help or over our hearts. I placed my hand over my heart and the healing began. I felt the presence of the entities and the energies sweeping through my body at a deep level, particularly centered in my heart and forehead. After half an hour, the session ended and we were guided to a receiving area where we were given instructions for the next twenty-four hours, then led to taxis to take us back to our pousadas. I went to my room and lay in bed, mostly asleep, for the next thirty hours.

For the first twelve hours after my surgery, I felt the entities continuing to work deeply within me. I had no trouble sleeping during this time. At meal times a fellow visitor at the pousada delivered meals to me, which I quickly ate before going back to sleep. The twenty-four hours seemed to go by quickly. I felt remarkably rejuvenated and clear after the surgery and my long rest. I continued to go to the Casa each day afterward for long sessions of meditation. The next week I had a second spiritual surgery. I was partaking in a profound spiritual healing at the Casa and was deeply appreciative.

Hundreds of entities, called brothers and sisters of light, aided in the spiritual healings at the Casa. One of the prominent ones was Santa Rita, a saint from fifteenth-century Italy. I was fortunate that she began to appear to me in my healing sessions. She had a deep devotion to God that I could sense and I cherished the moments when I was able to feel this from her. The first time I felt her presence, I became so lost in the feeling of her divine love for God that I became afraid, thinking I could not hold that amount of love and still remain in my body. Due to my fear, I came out of that experience. Later I realized that there is no limit to the love the human heart can hold.

One morning, as I was meditating at the Casa, I went into a deep place and again felt the presence of Santa Rita. At the same time, I became aware of another presence who I was surprised to realize was my wife Patricia in a beautiful angelic form. We looked at each other silently, nonverbally communicating an agreement to come together and have children to raise in a way pleasing to God. Coming out of meditation, I saw that I had been given a glimpse of what had occurred before I came into this life. Now I understood clearly why I had not become a monk. It was not because my gurus had found me unworthy, a sentiment I had carried with me for many years. Patricia and I had chosen to come into this world to serve God in a particular way, to devote ourselves to our spiritual lives in the context of our marriage, and to have children brought up in an atmosphere of love and service. Honoring our choice, my gurus had paved the way for this to occur.

Chapter 22

FURTHER GUIDANCE

I was so moved by my experience at the Casa that I went again the next year and the year after. I continued to have remarkable experiences there and returned home feeling cleansed and rejuvenated. However, the symptoms of chronic fatigue continued to recur and I came to understand that this was at least partially due to my inability to deal with the stress from my work.

After one of my trips to Brazil, I was introduced to a woman named Barbara who had been to the Casa several times and who was a channel for a disincarnate being named Aaron. Reading one of her books in which she channeled Aaron's teachings, I found that Aaron's words spoke directly to the difficulties I was having. Aaron reached enlightenment some five hundred years ago as a Buddhist monk in Thailand. Now, through Barbara, he was teaching the practices of Vipassana meditation from the Theravada Buddhist tradition. I was not interested in Buddhism or learning a new religious doctrine but

I was uniquely impressed by the simplicity and inherent truthfulness of Aaron's words. Finally, in May 2012, I reached out to Barbara and arranged to have a video session with Aaron.

Barbara was an older Jewish woman with an exceptionally kind appearance, her face reflecting her long years of spiritual work. She was deaf and used voice recognition software that transcribed my words onto her computer. We spoke for a short time and then she allowed Aaron to enter her body. Abruptly, I was speaking with an entirely different being. I found myself listening intently to Aaron's insights.

I informed Aaron that, despite my many years of spiritual practice, I still had difficulty controlling certain emotions such as anger, fear, and feelings of unworthiness. I was disappointed that I had not yet conquered these negative emotions.

Aaron offered me a unique perspective for dealing with difficult emotions. He shared the story of Milarepa, the Tibetan Buddhist master from the twelfth century, who lived in an isolated cave in the mountains, where he devoted himself to his practices for many years. One day he was meditating when a group of demons entered his cave. Astonished, he took out his sword and told them that only beings who practiced the Dharma could enter his cave. When the demons laughed at him and did not leave, he changed tactics and began teaching them the Buddhist teachings, the Dharma. This did not work either. Finally, in a flash of inspiration, he simply invited them in for tea. Disappointed in finding no opposition, all of the demons but one left. Now Milarepa calmly placed his head in this demon's mouth and said, "Eat me!" With this the last demon disappeared.

After hearing Aaron's story, I began inviting my lingering inner demons—my anger and feelings of unworthiness—in for tea. I began to get insight into their origins and how they shaped my perception. Most significantly, I saw I did not need to fight them or try to rid myself of them. As I was present with them without judgment, they slowly lost their power and for the most part dissolved on their own.

I became aware that a subtle thread of unworthiness had seemed to wind its way through my entire life. I asked Aaron about the source of this feeling. He explained that it was an inevitable part of the human condition. In choosing a human life, I had voluntarily agreed to limit the awareness of my inherent divinity, yet I nonetheless retained the memory of my divine nature and felt incomplete without it. I innately knew that I was more than I appeared to be. By choosing this limitation of human life, I was offered a profound opportunity to plumb deeper into the love I intuitively sensed within me. From Aaron's words I understood that feelings of unworthiness are common to all human beings. I began to see them as a catalyst for deeper spiritual work, not as an obstacle that had to be overcome.

One of the most difficult issues I shared with Aaron was the responsibility I felt for my clients and the anger that came up when I saw them being abused by our legal system. Aaron said, "Robert, you just cannot bear the suffering of others." At first I thought he was praising my sensitivity toward others. But soon I discovered that he was teaching me something subtler: that I could not bear the suffering of others because I feared for my own.

After many years of spiritual work, I believed that my deep faith allowed me to handle whatever came to me. But now I saw that I did not have complete faith and not all of the time. There were still elements of fear in me—fear that I would not receive what I needed in my life, that I would not be able to care for my myself and family, that things would not work out. These lurking fears subtly distorted my perception. I noted through my Vipasanna practice that my habit in reacting to these fears was to quickly try to fix things. I saw a lot of grasping in my attempts to quickly overcome what I perceived as my problems.

Similarly, when I observed others undergoing hardships, fearing that they could not deal with their own difficulties, I manifested the same need to quickly solve their problems. Having a concept of myself as a helper to all, I took on the weight of the suffering of others. It finally became apparent to me, through Aaron's guidance, that I could not fix everyone's problems and that I needed to have faith that others were equal to what they had to face.

In one incident, I sent one of my clients, an older Mexican woman, to Mexico to obtain her green card, which would give her lawful residence status in the United States. She had been illegally in the states for over twenty years but her husband and children were all U.S. citizens. We carefully followed the prescribed procedures that allowed her to legalize her status. However, when she went to the consulate in Mexico for her interview, she was denied because of a technicality. It was a mean-spirited and harsh decision.

I was extremely upset by these circumstances. Aaron suggested that I employ the Buddhist practice of *upekkha*, or equanimity, to be used in times when it is not in one's power to change a situation. The practice involves recognizing that all human beings have their own karma which they are responsible for and that much of this karma was outside of my power to change. For someone like me who made an implicit vow to serve all beings in my ashram days, upekkha was a difficult, often painful lesson to learn, but a necessary one.

In another session with Aaron, I shared with him a fear that I could not keep up with the needs of my family. Already in my late-sixties, I worried if I would be able to continue to support them. He said, "I want to teach you about manifesting." He then offered a simple practice in which each morning I began my meditation session with the following words: "I offer my service for the good of all, as much as I am able, and have faith that my needs will be met." At first as I repeated the words they seemed merely a verbal affirmation of what I wanted to believe. Yet after some days, I began to visualize internally how connected I was to the universe, how I was part of a vast matrix with energetic lines connecting me to everything within it. I saw that by offering my service to all, without attachment, the universe of its own accord responded to meet my needs. I saw clearly that I was not separate from the universe and it was not separate from me. I began to experience joy in how my own good intentions reverberated through the universe and were reflected back to me as abundance and grace.

From my many sessions with Aaron, I concluded that the issues most difficult for me are the same that plague all human beings: fears of not being worthy and of not receiving what I need in my life. I began to see these fears as mere thought patterns, ones I have been repeating throughout my life and, most likely, many lifetimes. They hold no inherent truth. Gradually I saw their power over me diminish. But realizing that I still had difficulty with these issues, even after many years of spiritual work, made me feel a sharp compassion for those who have never pursued a path of self-knowledge. How, I wondered, could they cope with these fears? Most likely by avoiding or denying them. I set an intention to try to help others, as best I could, understand their own inherent abilities to deal with these issues from a place of their own inner fullness.

Chapter 23

GOD, GURU, AND SELF ARE ONE

In October 2016 I took part in a Vipassana retreat offered by Barbara and Aaron on a sprawling communal farm in rural Indiana. It was the height of the fall season and the landscape was covered in the reds, oranges, and yellows of autumn. A river cut through the property as well as long, winding walking trails ideal for silent walking meditation. It was a beautiful setting and I was happy to have such a serene break from my daily work.

I had been studying with Barbara and Aaron for four years by this time and greatly appreciated what I learned from them. During one of the group sessions, Aaron complimented my progress in watching my emotions arise and subside from a place of detachment. Then he added, "But just watch a bit and see if there is any anger lurking in your mental landscape." I smiled and assured him that I would be observant. After our session I took a long walk through the fields to the river. It was a cool day and I was basking in the luxury of a beautiful autumn setting after so many years in Florida. Then suddenly my joy turned into something else. Anger started coming up and I was getting caught in it. It was an issue I had been dealing with for some time.

A few years back, Miraji had changed the structure of our ashram, making it smaller and essentially closing it to the public. The new policy made it almost impossible for me to visit. I sorely missed seeing her and visiting my old friends. So much of my spiritual life had been tied to being with her and the ashram environment. At one point Miraji told many who had been with her for years, "Your begging bowls are full. Now share your light with the world." Intellectually I understood that Miraji was helping us move on to the next stage of our spiritual process, enabling us to more fully realize our inherent independence and blossom in our own unique ways. However, emotionally I felt a sense of abandonment by this new policy.

Later in the day, in a group session headed by Aaron, I shared my feelings and recounted Miraji's words to our group. Aaron listened patiently and said, "Robert, perhaps you can understand your guru's words in another way. Perhaps you have been comparing the fullness of your begging bowl with the begging bowls of others?" Then he hesitated and said, "But I don't want to put words into your guru's mouth. Wait a moment and I'll ask your guru."

Surprised, I replied, "My guru is here?"

Aaron laughed and said, "Robert, your guru is always here!" After a pause he said, "Your guru says that you still don't understand that God, guru, and Self are one. This is why you are feeling so much pain about not being able to visit your ashram."

Hearing that Miraji was always present in my sessions with Aaron initially surprised me, but it shouldn't have. It was an essential teaching of our tradition that the guru is always with us. In fact when I first started my sessions with Aaron I had inwardly asked

Miraji to be with me through them. But not being able to be in Miraji's physical presence for a number of years had brought up doubts in me. Why wasn't she calling me to the ashram like she used to? Did she not care about me anymore? Had I done something wrong? It had become difficult for me to just watch these feelings of unworthiness arise and subside. I was caught in them.

After our group session, I retreated to the meditation hall to sit with my swirling thoughts and emotions. The practice of Vipassana is to be present with what is without judgment. So I sat and was present with myself as I watched my thoughts and feelings rise and fall, rise and fall. I watched the pain I felt at no longer being able to be with my guru. I saw that the feelings of unworthiness and abandonment that arose were age-old mental patterns that existed long before my relationship with Miraji. They were just thoughts and had no reality in themselves. I saw that my physical estrangement from my guru was a powerful catalyst that brought up these intense emotions so that I could see them for what they really were. I had projected unworthiness and abandonment onto so many situations in my life. Slowly the emotions began to fall away. What remained was my pure awareness and my awakened heart, full of love. Soon I was immersed in my essential Self, my heart of Love. This was what was real.

Guruji taught that a true guru is a vessel for a divine function, that of awakening people to their own inner divinity. For years I had been fortunate to be in the presence of two remarkable gurus, directly experiencing the divine energy that ceaselessly flowed through them. It was easy for me to see how God and guru were one. It was also easy to see why I had difficulty letting go of the desire to be with them. Yet now I clearly saw that I would always feel incomplete if I did not realize within that God and guru were always within me as my own Self.

Chapter 24

TWIN FLAMES

I t was the winter of 2017, a few months before my seventieth birthday. Something within was telling me I needed a change. My wife and I were now empty-nesters and she was working full time as a professor for an online university. I had been practicing immigration law for many years and saw myself repeating the same tasks over and over again. I was becoming uninspired by this aspect of my practice and sorely wished to offer others more than just legal advice. I had been committed to my spiritual life for many years. It was the core interest of my life. I now wanted to more fully share what I had learned with others.

Whenever I was in deep crisis mode, I consulted my trusty astrologer Diane, the same one who recommended John of God to me. As it seemed to always happen, I found I was undergoing a difficult Saturn transit, Saturn being the planet of limitation and hard life lessons. Diane looked at my chart and said, "You are ready for a change. Your life is appearing very difficult now so that you will take the initiative to make this change. You will be teaching others spirituality. Sometimes it takes a long time to make such a change, but for you it will happen very quickly." I was happy to hear these words. I truly wanted to dedicate my life to the teachings I had learned from my many years of spiritual practice.

In January 2018 I took another trip to the Casa of John of God. For the past years I had been going with a group led by Barbara, who combined meditation and group work with the healings offered by the Casa. I discovered that my healings were enhanced in the group context. Aaron asked us to consider what it would be like to be completely transparent in a group setting. Would we feel shame in allowing others to know our innermost thoughts and feelings? In these groups it was easy to let barriers fall away and come closer to this state of transparency. I saw major openings occur within our group when one member shared his or her innermost feelings before the others. Once one person opened up, a doorway seemed to open for all to go to a deeper level. This created a bond of love and trust between us that vastly enhanced our healing experiences.

In my sessions at the Casa, the entities worked on my heart chakra. In my years of meditation practice, my most profound experiences had been centered in the higher chakras—the crown and third eye chakras—where I experienced expansive spiritual states. Now, with the work on my heart chakra, I found that the spiritual insights from the higher chakras were being integrated into my physical reality. As the entities continued their work, I saw that my increased ability to be non-judgmental with myself was allowing my heart to open more and more. I was moving toward a state of transparency in which the barriers between myself and others were lessening.

Aaron often pointed out to me the protective shields I created around my heart to keep from being hurt. I saw that it takes faith, courage, and patience to look at these shields and slowly release them. Through this sometimes painful process I was becoming able to truly experience the unity that exists between myself and the world.

I stayed in Abadiania for three weeks on this trip and found that the extra week allowed me to unwind significantly. Still, I missed being home with Patricia and was looking forward to being with her. I was always aware of the special relationship we had based on our love and shared spiritual commitment. In Abadiania I was introduced to some literature about certain male and female beings who choose to evolve together, called twin flames. I found it a romantic concept, like soul mates, and wondered if it had any inherent reality.

On returning from the Casa, after many hours of travel, I found myself at home with Patricia. That night, after sharing my experiences with her, we lay in bed together and I felt a deep love for her. I was surprised to find that I had an intense desire to be intimate with her even though we were instructed at the Casa to avoid sexual contact for several days after our spiritual healings. Eventually, as we lay together entwined in our love, our hearts touching, I became aware of a divine light around us and recognized it as Santa Rita's presence. She seemed to like to remind me of the spiritual bond I shared with Patricia. Soon I was experiencing a white light above the two of us as we lay together, with bands of light encircling us, rising from below, winding around us to the vast white light above. There was so much love. I could not tell if we were one or two. I wondered at the message Santa Rita was sending me. Surely there was something holy about two beings dedicating themselves to God in a relationship of love and trust. It seemed this beautiful saint was again reminding me how special our relationship was.

Chapter 25

NEW INTENTIONS

It was early morning and still dark. A candle was lit on my altar in front of pictures of Guruji and Miraji. In meditation I asked God what the next step in my life should be. I knew I needed to slow down my law practice and engage more with spiritual teachings. Slowly I became aware of Guruji's presence and heard him chuckle and say, "Don't worry, you're coming to me!"

"Don't worry, you're coming to me!" I repeated these words over and over in the following weeks, trying to understand them. Was my time on this earth coming to an end, with Guruji drawing me to his divine presence? It did not feel that way. I was still healthy and in good shape for a seventy-year-old man. Was my consciousness going to merge into Guruji's in a state of enlightenment? Honestly, I did not feel that I was on the verge of sudden enlightenment. After weeks of contemplation, I concluded that Guruji was reminding me that, whatever choices I made in my remaining years, I would in the end be coming to him. It was the great gift of having such a guru.

Feeling free to make new intentions, I remembered a story by Tolstoy I had read years before, called "Father Sergius." Father Sergius was a young aristocrat in the Russian military, engaged to a beautiful noblewoman. Shortly before their wedding, he became aware that she had been a concubine of the tsar. Mortified, he hastily cancelled his engagement, quit the military, and retreated to a monastery to live a life apart from worldly cares. After living a monastic life for many years, he became famous as a healer and many came to him for his miraculous cures.

One day a beautiful, wealthy woman came to see him but only to satisfy her vanity by trying to seduce him. Her attempts failed when Father Sergius, unable to convince her to leave, took an axe and chopped off the little finger of his hand. He became even more famous after this story became widely known. However, soon after, a local man brought his mentally-disturbed daughter to Father Sergius for a cure. Alone with him in his healing chamber, the woman suddenly grabbed Father Sergius' hand and placed it on her breast. Taken by surprise, Father Sergius succumbed and ultimately had sexual relations with the woman.

Beside himself with shame and grief, Father Sergius cut his hair, abandoned his monk's robes and walked to the river, intent on ending his life. But, on entering the river, he was overcome with a vision of a woman he had known in his childhood. She seemed to be beckoning him to come to her. Reluctantly, Father Sergius abandoned his effort to end his life and walked the several miles to the farmhouse where he knew the woman lived.

The woman was greatly surprised to see such a celebrated figure come to her home. Father Sergius remained for a week observing how poorly the woman was treated by her husband and how, remarkably, she remained committed to the love and care of her children. He was deeply moved by her simple love. On departing Father Sergius understood the lesson he was to learn. He did not have to become anything special in his life. He had only to follow his heart and love and serve people to the best of his ability.

When I read this story, I knew it contained a message for me: I did not have to become anything special in this life. I just had to love and serve. Now I see again, in making intentions for the next part of my life, that I do not have to become anything other than what I am. I just have to make sure that whatever I do comes from love.

So it is that I write this book.

Acknowledgements

Writing about my spiritual journey, I have omitted much about my family life. In truth having a family and raising two beautiful children was an unexpected gift that has meant more to me than I can fully describe. Our family became a little community for the four of us with a wholeness and inter-activeness that brought joy and wonder to us all. Once, when my children were young, we were having breakfast at a lodge in Sedona, Arizona where the manager came up to us with tears in her eyes. She said she was moved by how Patricia and I always included our kids in our conversations and listened to them with so much respect. I'm grateful for that moment. It has always been an incredible joy to engage with my children and watch them experience life with their wide-eyed enthusiasm. When they went to college and Patricia and I finally took a vacation by ourselves, we could not keep from wondering how our kids would have experienced everything we were seeing and doing.

In my introduction I dedicate my book to the young seekers of today. But I also dedicate this book to my family who has meant so much to me over the past twenty-five years. My children are now adults with wonderful open hearts, forging their own unique paths in this world. My wife is a friend and helper to all she meets. The vision I had of her as an angelic being was accurate. I was told in Abadiania that Santa Rita usually appears to women and to those who help the downtrodden of our world. Somehow her visits to me have highlighted my relationship with Patricia and I believe it is because Santa Rita recognizes the spiritual strength Patricia has offered me during our years together.

Finally, I give thanks to my spiritual teachers, without whom my life would have been something quite different. It is difficult to find human beings who are so committed to uplifting others and who do so without any selfish motive. They are called saints in many traditions. Without their vibrations of divinity shining throughout this world, our planet would be a dreary place indeed. I bow my head to these great beings and offer myself to their teachings and service.

CPSIA information can be obtained
at www.ICGtesting.com
Printed in the USA
LVHW092134190222
711556LV00012B/75

9 781982 215569